Early reviews:

"This clearly writt... ...*aluable information....Usefu* ...*recommended for general readers."*
    American Library Association's BOOKLIST

"...Detailed, excellent advice on all aspects....Should be in the library...."
    NLS (Nassau County, New York, Library System)

Read what others have said about the 1984 edition of:

IT'S NEVER TOO LATE TO START OVER by Jo Danna
ISBN: 0-9610036-1-8, $10.95 (second edition to be available in 1986, $12.95) Pap.

"Much of this information is not only useful but is downright eye-opening....Highly recommended."
    American Library Association's BOOKLIST

"Rich with hard facts and sensible suggestions for an older person--or for that matter anyone--who is in the job market or considering a career change--I was especially impressed with the attention paid to the problems faced by older women..."
    Lydia Bronte, Ph.D., Carnegie Corporation of New York

"...of great interest and utmost value....an important public service...." Hon. Mario Biaggi, U.S. House of Representatives, Select Committee on Aging

WINNING
THE JOB INTERVIEW GAME
TIPS FOR THE HIGH-TECH ERA

Jo Danna, Ph.D.

PALOMINO PRESS
Briarwood, N.Y. 11435

WINNING
THE JOB INTERVIEW GAME
TIPS FOR THE HIGH-TECH ERA

Jo Danna, Ph.D.

Published by:

Palomino Press (SAN 241-5739)
86-07 144th Street
Briarwood, N.Y. 11435, U.S.A.

Copyright (c)1985 by Jo Danna
First Printing January 1986
Printed in the United States of America

Edited by Carl Danna

Book Cover: Robert M. Finke

Library of Congress Cataloging in Publication Data
Number 85-061451

Danna, Jo
Winning The Job Interview Game:
Tips For The High-Tech Era
Includes Index & Appendix
1. Personal & Practical Guides
2. Occupational & Educational Information
ISBN 0-9610036-2-6 Paperback

ABOUT   THE   AUTHOR

Jo Danna has degrees in psychology, anthropology and education. She earned her Ph.D. and M.A. from Columbia University, New York City and her Bachelor's Degree from Hunter College of the City University of New York. She is also a graduate of the Career Opportunities Institute, University of Virginia in Charlottesville.

TABLE OF CONTENTS

-1-
WHAT DO EMPLOYERS WANT?

The following criteria are not listed in order of priority. That's because what's most important to one employer may be less important or irrelevant to another.

DO YOU HAVE THE ABILITIES AND EXPERIENCE THE EMPLOYER NEEDS? Paid work and formal education aren't the only ways to acquire these. Besides, changes are coming so fast these days that new jobs often appear before there are any vocational or college level courses to prepare workers for them. Tell the employer about the job relevant skills and knowledge you have acquired from any of the following:

Home computer
Volunteer work
Part-time paid work
On-the-job training
Seminars and conferences
Trade and professional shows
Television educational series and documentaries
(e.g., computers, graphics, science, business topics)

ARE YOUR SKILLS AND KNOWLEDGE UP TO DATE? This is especially important in occupations where competition for openings is fierce. Knowing how to perform the tasks listed in a job description isn't enough these days. Job descriptions are continually being revised as a result of new knowledge and technologies. Even for entry level jobs, an awareness of innovations which improve productivity is enough to put you ahead in the game.

Only an ostrich can ignore the technological marvels which are reported daily in the media. The nation is still in the early stages of the electronics revolution. The really big changes are on the horizon.

ARE YOU WILLING TO LEARN NEW INFORMATION AND NEW WAYS OF DOING THINGS? In order to keep ahead of competitors, employers need workers who are prepared for the changes to come. Since new job openings often appear before there are any training programs for them, employers need workers who can learn as they go. They need generalists who are willing to learn a variety of new skills and knowledge, not specialists whose skills and knowledge will soon be obsolete.

An automobile company manager who applied for a job at a semiconductor company proudly told the interviewer that he had spent a full year studying how to sell padded roofs on Lincoln Continentals. Instead of being impressed, the interviewer was appalled. "The guy got into a five-minute dissertation on padded tops," he said in amazement.

LET THE INTERVIEWER KNOW YOU ARE AWARE OF WHAT'S HAPPENING IN YOUR OCCUPATION AND THE INDUSTRY AS A WHOLE. It isn't always necessary to take evening courses before applying for a job. Many employers have their own training programs or offer tuition reimbursement for workers who take courses to update their job skills.

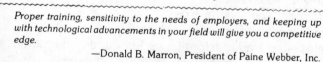

Proper training, sensitivity to the needs of employers, and keeping up with technological advancements in your field will give you a competitive edge.

—Donald B. Marron, President of Paine Webber, Inc.

♥ READ NEWS-PAPER AND MAGA-ZINE ARTICLES ABOUT INNOVA-TIONS IN YOUR OCCUPATION. Study the ads, too. In 1984, Apple Computer Company had several pages of ads in Newsweek which described their new MacIntosh Computer in detail.

♥ WATCH THE TV DOCUMENTARIES ON SCIENCE, TECHNOLOGY AND NEW MANAGE-MENT STYLES.

♥ LET THE INTERVIEWER KNOW IF THERE IS A COMPUTER, A WORD PRO-CESSOR OR A PRINTER IN YOUR FAMILY. (Even if you aren't the one who uses it.)

♥ TELL THE INTERVIEWER ABOUT THE CONTINUING EDUCATION COURSES YOU'VE TAKEN OR ARE PLANNING TO TAKE.

The following depict the benefits of being informed:

1. Bookkeeping is one of the occupations that are destined for the job junk yard. A bookkeeper who has played around with a computer spreadsheet, an accounting or income tax program, or has merely seen how one works, is way ahead of others who display their ignorance (and fear) of these popular programs.

2. A draftsperson who knows what CAD-CAM[*] means scores points over one who doesn't know the difference between this and Egg Foo Yung. He/She will score even higher by preparing for the coming obsolescence of this occupation with courses on computer graphics and design.

───────────

[*](Computer Aided Design - Computer Aided Manufacture)

3. At the very least, employers need typists who aren't scared by a computer keyboard. At best, they prefer to hire a typist who has learned to transfer his/her skills to word processing. All that's needed is a brief course (fewer than 10 days) at the "Y" or some work for a temporary placement agency which provides free training.

4. Two years after graduating from a prestigious art school, Gladys still couldn't find a job in the fine arts field. The waitressing and countless job rejections had brought her to the brink of despair. But she has a brother who is a computer freak. Without even trying, Gladys had absorbed computer terminology and an acquaintance of how computers work. She browsed through her brother's computer magazines, studying the ads on computer graphics and art, and reading occasional articles on the subject.

One day, as a prospective employer was showing her around the industrial art department, she saw a Lisa computer "in the flesh." Her eyes lit up. She also used some computer terminology which she had seen repeatedly in the magazines. This was all the employer needed to know in order to select her from among the many other job applicants who showed no knowledge of this important new technology and/or a fear of it.

It didn't matter that she hadn't taken any courses or even seen a computer graphics program in action. The employer had a training program which taught her all about it. Gladys will never again have to worry about finding a good paying job because she is on the leading edge of this new frontier of industrial illustration.

DO YOU KNOW A FOREIGN LANGUAGE? As the nation becomes increasingly multi-lingual, as the world becomes a global village as a result of modern communications, a second or third language is valued more than ever. The need for bilingual workers is greatest in cities where immigrant groups are settling in large numbers as well as in places like New York City and Washington, DC which have an international business and/or political orientation. Be sure to let the employer know you have these skills.

ARE YOU LITERATE? DO YOU HAVE GOOD COMMUNICATION SKILLS? A 1982 survey found that two fifths of over 2,000 employers reported reading deficiencies among office workers and over one half found poor mathematical skills among bookkeepers, technical workers and supervisors. In 1981, at least 34% of U.S. companies had to give remedial education to their employees.

Blue collar workers who are retraining for white collar jobs are especially in need of remedial education, cites one report. Many of these jobs require strong reading and math skills "which millions of workers don't have." Happily most of these older workers complete the retraining programs successfully.

Studies show that semi-literate and illiterate workers have lower productivity and more industrial accidents. In 1975 a herd of prime beef cattle died because a feed lot worker misread the package label and gave the cattle poison instead of feed. Several workers at a Westinghouse Electric Company plant were fired because they couldn't read the instructions on how to handle dangerous equipment.

Assuming your basic skills need improvement, you'll be ahead of the game by enrolling in a brief remedial course for adults or by doing some self-study. Contact the high school evening division for information.

♥ EVEN IF YOUR BASIC SKILLS ARE GOOD, A SHORT COURSE ON WRITING CAN BE THE SPARK THAT LAUNCHES A SUCCESSFUL CAREER. Among the most prized assets is the ability to write concise, coherent reports and memos. The way you write reflects the way you think. Are your thoughts logically arranged? Can you get to the point without drowning in a sea of irrelevances? If so, you are worth your weight in gold to an employer.

The chairman of a Fortune 500 company requires his managers to submit reports twice a month. He not only reads them, he grades them! Every candidate for a top job has to take a writing test!

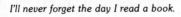

I'll never forget the day I read a book. —Jimmy Durante

ARE YOU CREATIVE? DO YOU LIKE TO SOLVE PROBLEMS? A December 1984 Report by the President's Commission on Industrial Competitiveness had an entire section devoted to the need to foster creativity in the workplace.

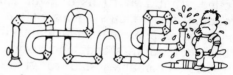

In times of rapid change, employers need workers who can help them solve new problems and find new solutions to old problems. They especially value workers who can anticipate problems before they even occur. A 1984 *Business Week* article asked why none of Atari Company's 7,000 employees failed to realize the video game craze was just a passing fad. Because of its failure to keep in touch with consumers, the company hit bottom seven years after leading the multimillion dollar video game boom.

The competition among employers to find creative talent is so great that some are offering dual career ladders and opening branch offices in choice areas which have scenic, recreational and cultural attractions. Xerox and IBM offer one year sabbaticals, paid membership in scientific and technical societies, and free post-graduate courses. It's not just the high-tech companies that are wooing creative people. Companies in other industries are offering lures such as an all-expense-paid weekend on the town or a trip to Europe.

ARE YOU WILLING TO TRAVEL? WILL YOU BE READY TO MOVE WHEN THE COMPANY RELOCATES OR OPENS A BRANCH IN ANOTHER CITY? You'll probably be asked this on a job application form or during the interview. If the job means a lot to you, answer "Yes." If you are willing to move to a place others turn down as America's "Siberia" you'll leap way ahead of other applicants who say "No."

Meg, who had recently graduated with honors in accounting, lost an opportunity to work for a "Big Eight" company because she balked at the ninety minute commute from her home in Long Island to Manhattan. But Manhattan is where the best promotion opportunities and highest pay are to be found. She settled for a lower paying, dead-end job closer to home.

PERSONALITY

Often, people sell themselves on the basis of personal qualities that are valued by employers, even though they lack some of the basic skills and knowledge requirements.

Many employers consider personal qualities to be more important than work experience. Studies show that a major reason for job dismissal is not poor performance but an inability to get along with coworkers, a sour attitude which casts a demoralizing spell, unreliability, and getting worked up easily over trivial matters. There's also the case of a bank employee who was warned to bathe more often or lose his job.

"Whatever your problem is, if you let it affect your relations with coworkers, it disrupts the harmonious workflow," says Josephine Lerro, former director of TempsAmerica. "Poor interpersonal skills account for about 65% to 75% of job terminations. Sometimes it isn't the employee's fault. Sometimes the problem lies with a supervisor who is difficult to get along with. Nevertheless, the employee must find ways to get along, otherwise that's not the place for him."

DO YOU HAVE A SENSE OF HUMOR? Psychological studies show that humor reduces hostility and the harmful effects of stressful situations. Humor is especially valued in jobs where there are many deadlines to meet and difficult people to deal with. It is also increasingly recognized as an important tactical weapon at shareholder's meetings, conventions, at formal and serious business functions, and as a management tool.

9

Furthermore, someone who spreads a bit of sunshine in the office is nice to have around. One young college graduate, physically less attractive and not much better qualified than other applicants for the job, was hired because his keen wit and sense of humor impressed the interviewer.

IS THERE ANYTHING IN YOUR BACKGROUND WHICH INDICATES DRIVE, INITIATIVE AND ACHIEVEMENT? Modern employers want workers who don't wait to be told what to do next and how to do the job better.

Do a self-assessment so you'll be able to tell the interviewer about your past efforts to contribute something beyond the stated requirements of a job or some other responsibility. See chapter five.

This is also where the home study course you completed or evening class you attended will add to your luster.

If you are changing careers, tell the interviewer how the abilities and responsibilities required in your previous occupation relate to the new one. Don't assume the interviewer will be able to see the connection. This is another way of demonstrating initiative.

Tell the interviewer about your voluntary work activities. The reason why job application forms ask for such aspects of your personal life is that they are indicators of your initiative and drive, your ability to get along well with others, and your creativity. One personnel recruiter looks especially at a candidate's voluntary work experience. "It shows you are involved, caring, energetic."

WILL YOU BE A RELIABLE EMPLOYEE? ARE YOU A CLOCK WATCHER? If so, maybe you're bored with the occupation you've chosen. See chapter five.

♥ ARE THERE LONG GAPS IN YOUR WORK RECORD? Never leave such gaps unexplained or the interviewer may wonder if you were ill, in prison or just plain lazy. Tell the interviewer about the many constructive activities in which you were involved (e.g., study, volunteer work, raising a family, part time or freelance work, travel, and caring for someone who needed your help).

♥ WILL YOU BE THERE WHEN THE BOSS NEEDS YOU? A reputation for being reliable is one of the greatest assets a young person can have, states a New York State Jobs Service manual. Employers are especially on the lookout for this quality in young people just entering the job market (as well as attitude, personal grooming and cooperativeness).

The manual cites the case of an attractive young woman who was selected for an airline's hostess training program. After only six months of active duty, she was fired. The reason? On several occasions she refused to take a flight, saying she didn't feel too well. Like the mail service, a scheduled flight must always go through, weather permitting. Only the most serious illness prevents pilots and hostesses from carrying out their assigned duties.

Another case cited is that of an 18 year old high school dropout who had fifteen different jobs in two years. Most of them lasted one or two weeks; the longest was three months! An employer would have to be charitable or desperate to hire someone with such a record.

The only way the young man can get out of this situation is to admit the problem was due to his immaturity, or that he had overwhelming family problems at the time. That's all in the past now. He's learned not to let his personal problems interfere with a job and he's more mature. The employer might be impressed with his humility and honesty and give him another chance.

If the employer shows no sign of budging, an offer to work on a trial basis at no pay or reduced pay might do the trick.

If the teenager has serious psychological problems, he should seek professional help before applying for yet another full time job. If he needs income, he can work at part time or temporary jobs. This will also give him the breadth of experience he needs to

11

develop a more mature attitude.

DO YOU HAVE A POSITIVE ATTITUDE?
Employers prefer to hire people who show enthusiasm for the job, the company, about life in general. They know that a worker who is satisfied and happy with the job is a more productive worker. The chief executive officer of a giant corporation says the most important thing he looks for is attitude. "I pick to promote only those who are positive. Those with negative attitudes don't have much of a chance."

A positive attitude helped a blind, 49 year old computer programmer get a job with DuPont Chemical Corporation. In fact, the company spent about $19,000 on adjustments for his handicap. Said a company spokesman, "It's a trivial sum...Just close your eyes and see how you feel... He's a tremendous influence on all of us with his attitude." [30]

A positive attitude implies having the strength of will to leave one's personal problems at home. It means being supportive of one's coworkers, and keeping one's gripes to oneself.

A negative attitude involves seeing the worst side of things, always criticizing the way things are done, gossiping about coworkers and tearing them down.

The New York State manual cites the case of an 18 year old high school graduate, tops in his class, who was fired one month after being hired. Although his work was good, he was dismissed because it got to the point where the supervisor and coworkers refused to have anything to do with him. He was a constant irritant. He frequently questioned management decisions despite the fact that he was ill informed, and he argued with coworkers about everything, including trivial matters.

♥ AVOID DISCUSSING YOUR PERSONAL, FINANCIAL OR FAMILY PROBLEMS DURING THE INTERVIEW so you won't be viewed as a whiner. Trying to win sympathy won't get you the job either. It will make the interviewer uncomfortable and want to terminate the interview prematurely.

♥ THERE'S NO NEED TO ACT APOLOGETIC ABOUT YOUR AGE OR LACK OF A COLLEGE DEGREE. Refer instead to your "hands on" experience and life achievements. If your skills are rusty, say you are planning to take adult education courses in order to upgrade them.

♥ IF YOU'RE A WOMAN RETURNING TO WORK AFTER MANY YEARS OF RAISING A FAMILY, FORCE YOURSELF TO CONVEY A POSITIVE, CONFIDENT ATTITUDE. "Far too many bring a hang-dog attitude in with them," says a Jobs Service counselor. "On your way to the interview, picture yourself as a competent employee rather than 'just a housewife.' Say to yourself, 'Your company is going to be proud to have me on board.'"

Take a course on assertiveness training if you need help in achieving the look of success. Contact the YWCA or other women's organizations listed in the Appendix. Contact the local college for more information.

THE WAY YOU ANSWER CERTAIN QUESTIONS SAYS A LOT ABOUT HOW YOU VIEW THE WORLD (e.g., "Tell me about some of the positive and negative aspects of your last job."). First mention the positive aspects--your accomplishments, relations with coworkers, job satisfaction, challenges and opportunities for developing new skills and knowledge, the work environment and management-worker relations.

As for the second part of the question, talk about trivial negative factors (e.g., "I would have liked a bigger work space."). Or, discuss negative features which highlight your best qualities (e.g., "There was too much socializing in the office and some of my coworkers resented the fact that I was more interested in getting my work done.")

DO YOU GET ALONG WELL WITH SUPERVISORS AND COWORKERS? The interviewer

Our computers are down, so we can't help you. All we have here is people.
—Manhattan telephone operator
answering a 411 call for information

13

can't tell by your appearance alone that you are a peach. Nor, for obvious reasons, can you be asked, "Do you get along well with people?" The interviewer can only rely on cues and indirect questions such as, "Tell me about your previous employer," or "Why did you quit your job?" or "Why were you dismissed?"

♥ NEVER SAY ANYTHING NEGATIVE ABOUT YOUR FORMER BOSS AND/OR COWORKERS, no matter how awful they were. Don't complain about the work conditions either, unless they were truly intolerable. In that case, begin by saying something nice about the company so that you project an attitude of fairness. One job seeker who had legitimate reasons for griping, later learned the interviewer and the employer he had bad-mouthed were in-laws.

♥ MENTION THE POSITIVE ASPECTS FIRST. "I liked my boss, but (...) " "The company had a good policy toward its workers, but (...)." Say how much you learned from the supervisor, how you appreciate the opportunity given you to work for the company. Describe the favorable aspects such as qualities of the work environment and your coworkers.

"WHAT WOULD YOU DO IN A SITUATION WHERE A CO-WORKER IS DIFFICULT; A WHINER, A PASS-THE-BUCK ARTIST, HOSTILE AND EASILY OFFENDED?" How you answer such a question reveals a lot about your attitude. You'll score points if you mention actions you would take which help increase team spirit, which show that you are a self-reliant, responsible person who doesn't pester a supervisor with continual tattling. Never say anything which humiliates or insults the co-worker. Don't say you'll get even or tell him or her off or refuse to have anything to do with that person.

Describe actions you would take which reveal your understanding of human psychology, your tact and leadership qualities (e.g., "The person is obviously misera-

He who slings mud loses ground.　　　　　—Adlai Stevenson

ble, so I'd be extra nice to him," or "He may lack self-confidence, so I'd compliment him, build up his self-esteem." or "He's probably a loner, so I'd have lunch with him. If that doesn't result in improvement, I'd offer some constructive criticism, but only after I build up his ego. Eventually, he'll come around or be fired. If not, I'd ask for a transfer."

ARE YOU A WORKAHOLIC? The work ethic is admirable but, some employers (not all) think too much is harmful. Some workaholics drive themselves to the point of neglecting their health, family and social life. This can lead to severe depression and/or drug or alcohol abuse. Other workaholics become tyrants who put so much pressure on others that valued subordinates or team members may quit.

ARE YOU A GOOD TEAM WORKER? This quality is more crucial in certain occupations and in certain organizations than others. See chapter three for more on this important topic.

WILL YOU CONTRIBUTE YOUR SHARE OF WORK AND IDEAS, AT THE VERY LEAST? At the most, will you be the sort of worker the employer can't get along without?

WILL YOU BE SUPPORTIVE OF YOUR SUPERVISOR AND CO-WORKERS? Putting a supervisor (who may be highly valued by the boss) in a bad light by complaining about him/her to coworkers or by going over his head, is frowned upon. It also reveals ignorance about the company's organizational structure--who is supposed to report to whom. An employee who finds ways to resolve differences privately with a supervisor scores points.

ARE YOU OVERLY AMBITIOUS? *MONEY* magazine describes a new breed of ambitious overachievers who ignore the needs of coworkers and goals of the

Do Unto Others, Then Run. — Benny Hill

company in their mad rush to get to the top. "Those who make a habit of cutting their colleagues' throats usually end up cutting their own," cites a study by Chester Wright of the Federal Office of Personnel Management.

WILL YOU BE LOYAL TO THE COMPANY AND ITS MANAGEMENT? Employers won't tolerate open criticism of superiors and the company. An employee of Jersey Central Power & Light Company's nuclear plant lost his job after he wrote a letter to a newspaper stating his opposition to the nuclear industry. He sued, but an arbitrator ruled the company did not have to retain an employee with such an attitude. His actions could jeopardize the company's "image" and have a big impact on other workers' job security.

They won't tolerate employees discussing personal grievances with other workers. (There are safer ways to do this in situations where other workers also suffer from legitimate abuses.)

Also on their hit list is talking about company secrets at a local hangout where a rival company's employees may overhear. Companies have gone bankrupt because a blabbermouth revealed plans for a new project which a competitor "happened" to overhear. Companies have been known to plant spies in local bars and restaurants and at sporting events where the employees of rival companies are known to hang out.

ARE YOU A RESPONSIBLE PERSON?
"Tell me about your strong points." Questions like this offer an opportunity to display your sense of responsibility. For example, did you help out a previous boss during a time of emergency or opportunity by skipping lunch, working longer hours or on weekends? Did you save an important account for your employer by meeting a deadline? Cite examples from your personal life as well.

"Tell me about your weak points." Slant your description of any "weak points" so that your sense of responsibility and work ethic shine through.

Never try to make the interviewer feel sorry for you. Instead, demonstrate your strength of will in overcoming difficulties.

NEVER MAKE EXCUSES FOR ANY SHORT-COMINGS. For example, if you arrive late for the interview or miss it entirely because you forgot to put it on your calendar, you'll lose points if you make excuses:

"I was sick."
"I ran out of gas."
"My car broke down."
"The train was late."

The interviewer will wonder why, if you want the job badly enough, you didn't prepare for such contingencies by leaving home an hour or so earlier. Why didn't you plan alternate ways to get to the interview? Why didn't you make sure the car was in working order?

A young copy writer phoned an advertising agency a day before the interview for directions on how to get there by car. Yet, she arrived 15 minutes late. Then, when the interviewer asked what happened she replied, "The secretary gave me the wrong directions." Her response showed:

1. Poor teamwork by putting the blame on the secretary.

2. Lack of responsibility. Why didn't she leave home at least a half hour earlier in case of an emergency or a wrong turn? Why did she rely on someone else to get the directions? Can't she read a map?

WILL YOUR ON-THE-JOB BEHAVIOR CONFORM TO THE COMPANY'S CODE OF ETHICS AND PROPRIETY? The president of a major corporation hit the ceiling when he spotted a girlie magazine on a manager's desk. An oversight like this can put an employee out of the race for a promotion.

♥ DO NOT CARRY GIRLIE MAGAZINES, COMIC BOOKS, TRASH NOVELS OR SENSATIONAL NEWSPAPERS TO THE INTERVIEW. Bring, instead, the type of literature which will enhance your overall image and carry it so the interviewer is bound to see it.

A trade or professional journal; a textbook in your

field; a major newspaper such as *The New York Times*, *Wall Street Journal*, *Washington Post*; and magazines such as *Time, Business Week, MONEY, High Technology, Info-World and Compute*,--all add to your luster.

♥ **DON'T FLIRT WITH THE INTERVIEWER OR GIVE ANY HINT OF A FLIRTATIOUS PERSONALITY.** Many employers feel that office romances upset the delicate balance of relationships among the workers. "We would like a person to project a certain image. Part of that is to be responsible," said a personnel director in describing the company's disapproval of an extramarital affair between two employees.

♥ **IF YOU'RE A WOMAN,** don't wear anything suggestive of the bedroom look.

♥ **WATCH YOUR BODY LANGUAGE.** You'll send a subtle, sexual signal which is inappropriate to a job interview if you sit with your legs apart, sit too close to the interviewer or touch the interviewer (except for a handshake).

DOES YOUR OVERALL APPEARANCE REFLECT THE DESIRED COMPANY IMAGE? Dress for the interview in the style preferred in the company. Look as though you fit in with the crowd. Research shows that people prefer to be with those who resemble them most in personal style, interest and appearance.

DO YOU HAVE THE PHYSICAL AND MENTAL STAMINA TO DO THE JOB WELL? In an effort to curb soaring health costs and raise worker productivity, U.S. companies in 1984 spent millions of dollars on programs to improve their employees' health. The goals of these programs include:
>   No smoking
>   Weight control
>   Improved nutrition
>   Control of alcoholism and drug abuse
>   Counseling on family and marital problems

♥ DON'T SMOKE UNLESS THE INTER-VIEWER SMOKES (WHICH IS UNLIKELY). If you are offered a cigarette, it may be to test whether you are a smoker. More employers these days are refusing to hire smokers.

♥ DON'T MENTION ANY HEALTH PROB-LEM which does not interfere with your ability to do the job. On the other hand, if you have a chronic prob-lem which will affect your job performance, you shouldn't be applying for the job. There are other opportunities where you'll be more comfortable and happy.

♥ "YOU CAN NEVER BE TOO THIN OR TOO RICH," said Wally Simpson. Obesity kills more Americans than any other health problem, say the experts. It also handicaps a person in the race for jobs and promotions.

Employment recruiters say obese persons are rarely promoted from lower management ranks, and among equally qualified job candidates the one who is trim is more likely to be hired. In general, overweight job seekers are viewed as health risks and less productive workers. They are even barred from some professional or trade training programs such as nursing and police work.

DO YOU HAVE ANY PERSONAL OR FAMILY PROBLEMS WHICH MIGHT INTERFERE WITH YOUR JOB? Employers want workers who can leave their problems at home. Workers who cannot deal with their personal problems are less productive and help increase costs.

The recent, dramatic increase in the number of families run by single parents concerns some employers. They worry that job performance will suffer as a result of emotional stress and an inability to separate family and work. One company admitted firing several employees be-cause the persistent emergency phone calls from home resulted in sloppy work.

Nevertheless, there are many persons in positions of responsibility who successfully apply their planning, organizing and administrative skills to managing home and work demands. Employers value such skills and sense of responsibility.

♥ DON'T REVEAL ANY PERSONAL PROBLEMS WHICH MAY MAKE EXCESSIVE DEMANDS ON YOUR ENERGY AND TIME, nor give yourself away with comments like these: "May I take ten days off next month when my son is scheduled to have his appendix removed?" or "My mother needs to go for physical therapy twice a month. Is it possible to rearrange my work schedule so I can take her?"

♥ IF THE INTERVIEWER BRINGS UP THE MATTER, BE READY TO EXPLAIN HOW YOU HAVE ORGANIZED THINGS SO THERE WON'T BE ANY INTERFERENCE WITH YOUR WORK. Say you have arranged for day care, help from relatives or neighbors, or a part time housekeeper or nurse. This is a good time to impress the interviewer with your organizing and administrative talents.

IS YOUR PERSONALITY COMPATIBLE WITH THAT OF THE ORGANIZATION? See chapter five for more on this important, new interest among management circles.

IS YOUR PERSONALITY COMPATIBLE WITH THE JOB YOU'RE APPLYING FOR? Certain occupations require specific cognitive-personality traits. For example, salespersons must be outgoing and competitive, and enjoy being with people. Computer programmers, on the other hand, should be somewhat introverted, non-competitive, analytical minded, and enjoy solving problems.

The Wall Street Journal reports how increased competition in the health care industry is changing some criteria used to select new employees. In an effort to improve services, hospitals are teaching human relations and communications skills in order to get nurses and other employees to smile more and show more warmth. One hospital, for example, has seminars on "niceness" for its employees after a survey showed patients gave it poor grades for its impersonal environment.

WHAT TURNS OFF EMPLOYERS?

IGNORING THE NEEDS OF THE ORGANIZATION: Employers are in business to make a profit. Your answer to such questions as, "Why do you want to work for us?" reveals whether you understand this.

APPEARING SELF-CENTERED: "Because I like to work with people," or "It's only 15 minutes from my home," or "I like the salary." A one-sided "What can you offer me?" attitude is a turn-off when you haven't even been offered the job. The time to negotiate is after an offer is made.

Pitch your sales talk to the needs of the organization. Do your homework first so you will be able to describe how you'll be a valuable addition to the team. (See chapter two.) In the competition between two equally qualified candidates, the one who knows the most about the organization will be hired. Show that you have made an effort to learn more than the run-of-the mill job seeker knows.

Some experts say the first thirty seconds are the most crucial for capturing the interviewer's attention. It's easier to do this if you know yourself well enough to describe how you'll be able to meet the employer's needs.

This information will also help you to avoid the worst sin of the job interview--appearing fuzzy minded about what you want and are qualified to do. Saying, "I'll take anything," can be forgiven in an eighteen year old but not in a thirty year old.

LACKING SELF-CONFIDENCE.

HOLDING POLITICAL, RACIST OR SEXIST VIEWS WHICH MIGHT EMBARRASS THE COMPANY. Are you a member of a controversial organization which may tarnish the company's public image and alienate clients?

REVEALING ON AN APPLICATION FORM OR DURING THE INTERVIEW YOUR MEMBERSHIP IN A CONTROVERSIAL ASSOCIATION. Although the law generally protects employees from being fired because they belong to a controversial organization (e.g., Gay Rights, Gray Panthers, Socialist Party), it cannot tell an employer to choose one job applicant over other, equally qualified applicants.

However, the law may not protect workers whose outside activities offend their employers. A worker who was fired when his employer learned he was active in the Ku Klux Klan filed a lawsuit claiming unlawful discharge. A Federal judge dismissed his case on the grounds that workers who belong to such hate groups cause trouble and lower morale in the workplace.

INDULGING IN AFTER-HOURS ACTIVITIES AND BEHAVIOR THAT WOULD TARNISH THE COMPANY'S IMAGE. The original Henry Ford hired detectives to visit local bars and spy on employees who drank too much. Today, more employers are investigating the backgrounds of job candidates before hiring them. Some check for credit history and court and arrest records. Some even require a urinalysis test for drug and alcohol abuse.

Many of the criteria discussed in this chapter were obtained from numerous newspaper, magazine and journal articles; others from interviews with personnel specialists. To test the "new wave" criteria further, a survey of several high technology companies was made. The human resource managers were asked to list a set of given criteria in order of importance to their company. The results support the published data with a few exceptions.*

For the position of SECRETARY, the criteria rated most important were:
"Adapts easily to change"
"Up-to-date knowledge and skills"
"Works well independently"
"A sense of humor."

"Creativity"
"Physical appearance."
"Works well in teams"

Least important for this position were:
"Generalist training"
"Loyal" (stays with same employer 7 or more years)
"Specialist training"

For a TECHNICAL/PROFESSIONAL position, the criteria rated most important were:
"Up-to-date knowledge and skills"
"Creativity"
"Adapts easily to change"
"College degree or higher" or
"Specialist training"
"Works well independently"
"Works well in teams"

Rated as least important for these positions were:
"Physical appearance"
"Loyal" (stays with same employer 7 or more years)
"Generalist training"

* The sample size was not large enough to constitute a scientific test.

BEFORE GOING ON A JOB INTERVIEW, GET THE FACTS. It will pay off in the following ways:

You'll be able to convince employers that hiring you will be in their best interest.

The interviewer will be impressed by how well informed and up-to-date you are in your field.

Your questions will be more relevant, will boost your rating, and help you make a wiser decision.

Your needs and those of the employer will be clearer. This will improve the logic and clarity of your answers. You'll know, for example, the critical details to emphasize and the language that's appropriate to the occupation and industry.

If you're a blue collar worker retraining for a white collar job, you'll have a better understanding of how the new work environment differs from your former one (e.g., relations with coworkers and management, dress code, language, and expected code of behavior).

It will also fatten your mailing list of employers to contact.

IF YOU'RE ASKED, "WHERE DO YOU EXPECT THIS JOB TO LEAD?" (or, "Where do you see yourself in this company five years from now?"), you'll be able to speak in terms of job families. These include a range of positions you'll be qualified to fill. You'll also be able to discuss the company's goals and your plans to expand and update your skills and knowledge in accordance with these goals.

"WHAT ARE YOUR WEAK POINTS?" Knowledge of the job responsibilities and the company will help you tailor your answers so as to highlight your best points. For example, if the job involves traveling and dealing with a variety of people, you might say how much you dislike being cooped up in an office, doing the same routine over and over. You can point out how much you enjoy the challenge of dealing with different kinds of people.

OR, IF YOU ARE ASKED, "WHAT WILL YOU CONTRIBUTE TO OUR ORGANIZATION?", you will know in detail how your qualifications meet the job's requirements and more. You'll reveal your knowledge of potential problems faced by the organization that result from changes in consumer needs, technology and other assaults on its established way of doing things.

Suppose you're applying for a job in a textile mill. You've been reading about the cheaper foreign imports which will deluge the U.S. market. You'll casually mention that the Japanese have cut costs and improved quality by using worker participation, and you'd be very interested in being part of that should the employer introduce this new management technique. (You know what "worker participation" is because you were smart enough to buy this book.)

Or, if you know that a rival company is planning to install computer aided design and manufacturing, you might casually mention it and your interest in computers or the evening course you're planning to take in that field.

I've learned always to ask myself these questions: What am I doing? Why am I doing it? What is the wisest thing to be doing?

— Eleanor Roosevelt

THE MORE YOU KNOW ABOUT AN EMPLOYER, THE LESS LIKELY YOU'LL TURN DOWN A GOOD JOB OFFER THAT INITIALLY FALLS SHORT OF YOUR EXPECTATIONS. Sometimes it pays to accept a lower salary or job title if:

1. The employer has a policy of promoting from within.

2. It offers the opportunity to acquire "hands on" experience which often means more to employers than an academic degree.

MONEY magazine writes of a New York University graduate whose goal was to be an advertising account executive. After months of futile job hunting, she accepted a secretarial job with a top firm. This was a smart move. She was placed in the department where she would see, first hand, what others in her hoped-for position were doing. And it gave management the opportunity to know her, like her and evaluate her potential. (She must have read about female executives who began as secretaries in the very same companies they now direct.)

The New York Job Service reports the case of a high school graduate who had studied house wiring and motor repair. He was referred to a public utility company for a trainee job which would lead to mechanical and technical positions. Foolishly, he turned down the offer because for the first six months he would be a messenger boy.

Had done his homework, he would have known the company has a policy of using the delivery job to test new employees fresh out of high school. An employee's ability to get along with coworkers and follow instructions, his reliability, and other personality related qualities mean as much to an employer as having the right skills.

*I*T'S EVEN MORE IMPORTANT TO GET THE FACTS ON A SMALL BUSINESS, ESPECIALLY A FAMILY OWNED ONE. The lure of working for a small business is hard to resist.

There is more opportunity to gain valuable experience in many aspects of the business. Relations with coworkers and owners are informal. Work hours are more flexible. And, if the business grows, so can your career.

However, flexible hours may mean overtime work for which you won't get paid if the owners are short of cash. The goldfish bowl atmosphere means a greater likelihood of personality clashes. If the boss is a tyrant, there's no place to hide and no supervisor to turn to for comfort and advice as in a large company. Furthermore, 80% of new businesses fail within five years, reported the Small Business Administration in 1985. In the volatile high-tech industries, the likelihood of failure is even higher.

FACTS YOU NEED TO KNOW ABOUT A SMALL BUSINESS INCLUDE THE FOLLOWING:
- ♣ The people you will be working with
- ♣ The financial health of the business
- ♣ Its growth prospects

Although it's not so easy to find information about small, newly established businesses, it's not impossible. Here are some sources:

Local newspapers usually carry articles and brief notices about them. They also maintain files on local employers. Look in newspaper indexes (e.g., *The New York Times Index*). If the newspaper is too small to have a bound index, ask the librarian to help you locate recent articles or phone the newspaper.

Standard & Poor's Index contains useful facts about many (not all) businesses, some with as few as two employees (e.g., address and phone number, names of officers, main business activity, dollar volume of business.)

Personal contacts are the best source of inside information--someone you know (or knows someone) who works for the small company you're interested in.

A phone call to the business editor of the local newspaper might pay off. If he/she does not have the

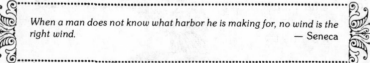

When a man does not know what harbor he is making for, no wind is the right wind.
— Seneca

answers to your questions, ask where you can get the information.

For more general information, browse through career guides which have sections on small businesses. Be sure these are up to date. A good guide is Mark O'Brien's *The MBA Answer Book: A Career Guide For the Person Who Means Business,* (Prentice Hall). It discusses what to look out for and where to find answers to questions such as these:

Have any bankruptcies been filed?

Does the business have a "shady" reputation?

Is the percentage of long term debt to total capital more than 20% to 25%?

Are new plant and equipment being paid with profits, with the proceeds of selling its stock, or with bank loans?

If you still have doubts about a particular employer, you can ask about the company's financial situation and growth prospects at the interview. It is your right to have any doubts cleared up. First, be sure they want to hire you.

L EARN ALL YOU CAN ABOUT THE OCCUPATION: job responsibilities, working conditions, education and training requirements, pay range, where the job leads and the personality characteristics that best fit the job.

Ask people you know who are in it.

Look it up in the U.S. Department of Labor publications listed in the Appendix.

Try to get hold of a job description used by a local employer. The nearest Job Service office or a school or college placement office may be able to help you. Job descriptions for each occupation in a well-run organization may also be found in the company manual or employee handbook.

A JOB DESCRIPTION lists the duties of an employee, the education and experience required, and criteria used to evaluate work performance. You'll also find it useful for evaluating your own past work performance. This will be/ helpful when answering such questions as "In what ways are you qualified for this job?" or "What are your strong points?"

*L*EARN AS MUCH AS YOU CAN ABOUT THE INDUSTRY YOU HOPE TO WORK IN. If you are a secretary, for example, decide whether you would rather work in the health care, education, entertainment, manufacturing, cable, TV, financial, publishing, or some other industry.

It's important to know this because job opportunities vary according to how well an industry is doing compared to other industries. You might learn, for example, that secretarial jobs in the local steel mill are scarcer than hen's teeth while the real estate, financial and software manufacturing industries are putting out the red carpet for you.

Professional associations are a good source of information on the industry you want. Look in *The Encyclopedia of American Associations* for addresses and names of persons to contact. See the Appendix for other sources.

*N*ARROW DOWN YOUR CHOICE OF EMPLOYERS TO CONTACT. Establish a list of priorities from "must have" to "must avoid." Screen them according to their future prospects. This is important in the volatile high-tech industry where it's here today and gone tomorrow.

THEN DIG FOR SOME HARD FACTS ABOUT EACH EMPLOYER ON YOUR LIST. Here are some suggestions on what to find:
1. Business activities
2. Number of employees
3. Training and continuing education benefits
4. "Personality" (or culture) of the organization
5. Frequency of job performance and salary reviews.

The biggest sin is sitting on your ass.

— Florynce Kennedy

6. Major divisions and departments, who does what, who reports to whom, who outranks whom: This is known as an organizational chart. It's like a map which displays such information at a glance. You'll even be able to locate your job category on the company's "totem pole."

7. Policy on promotions (whether it promotes from within or prefers to hire outsiders.): For example, you may discover many of the the top level managers and officers are Ivy League graduates or they come from Texas. This gives you a clue to your chances for promotion in the company.

8. Turnover rate (especially in the department and job category you want): If there has been a series of resignations in the department, you'll want to find out why before you get stuck with a workaholic or despotic manager.

9. Layoff policy: Some companies use lay offs as a last resort when a recession hits. They prefer, instead, to retrain employees and place them in other jobs or reduce the payroll through retirements and resignations.

10. Names and phone numbers of officers, including the personnel director and head of the section where you hope to work.

11. If you're a woman (or a minority group member) whose goal is to attain a top management or executive level position, find out how many others like you are in the top levels of the organization.

12. The company's future plans and prospects: Note any new products or services being planned, new contracts the company is bidding on, new fields it plans to enter, new acquisitions.

A recent college graduate who was rejected on his first try at the main office of a large company learned they were planning to open a branch in another state. He phoned the interviewer and said he was willing to move "anywhere" to be a member of their team. Despite the fact that he lacked the experience they wanted, he was hired. The reasons?

He was persistent.

He had done his homework.

He was available at the right time.

He showed his preference for the company.

13. Find out whether job openings within the organization are posted so all employees can learn about them. Elizabeth Fowler (*The New York Times* "Careers" column) cautions that supervisors sometimes block a worker's attempt to move into a different job classification by withholding information on job openings within the company. They do this because they don't want to lose workers they've spent years training. Posting all job openings prevents this from happening.

14. Get the facts on the company's current financial health and how it compares with others in the industry. This may prevent what happened in the following horror stories from happening to you. Be especially on the lookout for impending mergers. This could lead to a shakeout in which employees, especially those at the higher levels, will be dismissed.

A 60 year old industrial designer who had not been able to find a job in over a year found a $50,000 a year dream job only to lose it five months later when his company was acquired by a larger corporation.

"A.R.," an electronics engineer, was hired by the computer manufacturing division of a large, well known corporation. If he had done his homework before accepting the job, he would have known the division was being kept afloat by the profits of another and would soon be eliminated.

Among other problems that might occur, besides operations that are losing money, are costly lawsuits against the company. A chemistry graduate who had hoped to work for a particular chemical corporation, learned in the nick of time there was a Federal civil action and numerous individual lawsuits filed against the company because it had dumped hazardous wastes in a public area over a period of years.

DO A SELF-ASSESSMENT to determine whether you have the interests, abilities and personality traits required for the job. It will also help you decide which type of organizational "personality" you're most compatible with. See chapter three.

PLAN YOUR RESEARCH STRATEGY: It takes time to get the information you need. A good

plan will help you save much time and
effort, and your data will be in more
usable form.

GET ORGANIZED:
Bring index cards or a looseleaf note-
book with dividers to the library. Keep a
separate section for each occupation,
industry and employer you're interested in
   As you read, jot down the facts under one or more of
the headings listed below. You might think of others
which are relevant to your needs.
   Pay range
   Persons to contact
   Working conditions
   Current need for workers
   Where and how you fit in
   Buzzwords used in the industry
   "Personality" of the organization
   On-the-job training opportunities
   Education and training requirements
   Where the best job opportunities are located
   Specific departments where your assets are most
   needed

   In the section or index card for each employer you
plan to contact, reserve space for the following: dates
resumes were sent, phone calls made, letters received,
and names of persons contacted. Also, leave some room for
jotting down important points covered in your interviews.

KEEP A FACT FILE of articles from newspapers and magazines about the industry, occupation and
companies which interest you. You'll make a better impression at the interview; the more you know, the better
you can describe how your credentials will benefit the
firm.

JOT DOWN THE BUZZWORDS used by insiders in
the occupation and industry, and memorize them. Use them,
discretely, wherever they are appropriate, in your letters, resume and interviews. Even if you aren't applying
for a professional, managerial or technical job, the

33

judicious use of saavy terminology such as "bottom line," "worker participation," "quality circles" or "software" makes you appear up-to-date. This is especially important for older job seekers.

Be careful not to overdo it, or you may appear to be an ass!

IRS REGULATIONS allow you to deduct the expenses of looking for a job. Keep a record of all costs for travel to and from an interview, phone calls made, resume preparation and printing, employment agency fees, parking meters, postage and expenses involved in your research. If you find a job which requires moving out of town, these expenses are also deductible.

WHERE TO FIND INFORMATION ON EMPLOYERS: The following sources of information contain all you need and more. Don't be scared off by the enormous amount that is available. Much of what is in these sources overlaps. There's no need to delve into each one. Be selective. Stop when you feel you have enough information.

Bookstores
Newspapers
Public library
Personal contacts
Magazines, journals
Job Service Office
Stock market trends
Better Business Bureau
Informational interviews
U.S. Department of Commerce
Conventions and trade shows
Securities Exchange Commission
Company manuals and annual reports
Trade and professional associations
School/College career counseling office

THE PUBLIC LIBRARY has much of the information you'll need. Look in the card catalogue for books, indexes and periodicals on occupations, employers, and industries you are considering. If you can't find what you want, ask the librarian.

The reference section has subject indexes which direct you to articles in periodicals and books which the library may have on its shelves or on microfilm, or get through interlibrary loan or computer search. In some reference books, you'll find the addresses of employers you are interested in as well as the latest happenings in your chosen occupation and industry.

For example, *The New York Times Index* is a subject listing of articles published by the newspaper. *The Business Periodicals Index* lists articles in a wide variety of business and technical magazines such as *InfoWorld*, *High Technology*, *Journal of Marketing*, *Telecommunications*, *Fortune*, *Business Week*, *Forbes*. You'll also find company manuals, annual reports and brochures from the larger firms and, possibly, the smaller, local ones.

Then, check the vertical file (clippings, pamphlets arranged by subject). Look for a careers file or section. If you can't find what you want, ask the librarian. Many libraries will research, at no charge, any topic that's difficult to find information on. You may even be able to get the information you need over the phone.

In some states the public libraries have Education and Job Information Centers (EJIC) which enable you to get information and professional advice with the least amount of time, money and effort. They were established as a public service during the recent recession.

These centers have business directories, magazines and newsletters; samples of self-administered interests tests which you may find useful in doing a self-assessment; directories of career counseling and employment services; tips on resume writing, and more. Some also provide professionals who administer and interpret psychological tests for career counseling.

SCHOOL AND COLLEGE CAREER COUNSELING OFFICES have a reference library which contain reports on the job market, directories of employers in private industry and government, books on occupations and job hunting tips. On appointment, they also administer and interpret aptitudes and interests tests to help you decide on an appropriate occupation.

If you want specific information about a local employer or industry and the local pay range for the type of job you want, make an appointment to speak with a counselor.

Generally, the services are offered to students and alumni only, even years after graduation or attendance. If you have recently taken a course as a part time student, you may also be eligible. If you attended many years ago, it's not too late to have your dossier updated and registration reactivated.

During the recent recession, some colleges and universities began offering counseling services and the use of their libraries to all unemployed residents of the community.

PROFESSIONAL AND TRADE ASSOCIATIONS AND UNIONS provide up-to-date information on job openings, salaries, and training requirements. They are also a good source of information on a particular industry. If you meet the membership requirements and pay a fee, you can have your name registered in the central job bank and receive their newsletter or journal.

If you are not eligible for membership, you may be able to find their publications in the library. These are among the best sources of current information on employers and on job market events in the industry.

THE U.S. BUREAU OF INDUSTRIAL ECONOMICS also provides information on market trends and business forecasts for any industry. Contact: The Industry Publications Division, Trade Development, Room 4424, Herbert C. Hoover Building, Washington, D.C. 20230.

CONVENTIONS, CONFERENCES AND TRADE SHOWS are valuable for making personal contacts and learning about state-of-the-art developments in your occupation and industry. You'll probably carry home a shopping bag full of literature which have all kinds of interesting information including the latest buzzwords. Some admit only members and their guests. Others accept any interested person who pays the entrance fee.

Take advantage of the opportunity to speak with employers' representatives.

It's possible to get the information presented at these events without attending them. However, you'll miss the personal contacts and the excitement. The proceedings, lectures and names of company representatives are usually published. Contact the main office of the sponsoring association.

You can look up the dates of local gatherings in the newspaper and by phoning the local Chamber of Commerce. The *Directory of Conventions*, journals and the association's newsletter are other sources for learning the calendar of events.

PERSONAL CONTACTS can give you inside information about a particular employer and occupation which you won't find in print. Here are some of the questions for which you might be able to find answers:

What is the dress code?

Where does the job lead?

Describe the work environment.

What's the best way to get hired?

What do you like most/least about the work?

What are the reasons for a high turnover rate?

How do the employees feel about the company?

What kind of person do they prefer to hire?

What do you like most/least about the company?

Is the company having any particular problems and difficulties?

What is the turnover rate, especially in the job or department you're interested in?

Why did the previous worker leave? If the vacancy is

the result of a dismissal, learn the reason so you'll know what to avoid saying and what to highlight in the interview. For example, if the person was unreliable, you'll focus on your reliability.

Personal contacts include the following:

Someone you know who works, or has worked, for the employer.

Persons who are already employed in your chosen occupation.

Counselors in the local school or college career planning and placement office. They generally have long-standing contacts with local employers (as well as those in other communities). They are also good sources of information on large companies which come around regularly to recruit their best graduates.

School or college alumni who work in your chosen occupation or industry and may know about the employers on your list. Ask for a list of graduates (names, phone numbers and addresses) who are willing to help a fellow alumnus. Don't be shy about phoning or writing to them, even if you don't know them. The old school tie is almost as strong as a blood tie. In fact, in our society, it's probably stronger.

Someone you know who knows someone else with the information you need.

Telephone the person who writes the local newspaper's business column and ask for information about a local employer, pay ranges and working conditions. If you ask for this information over the phone, rather than in writing, you are more likely to get some off-record advice.

If you don't have personal contacts, find out where the company personnel regularly eat lunch or hang out, and eavesdrop.

INFORMATIONAL INTERVIEWS are recommended by some career counselors in order to learn more about a particular occupation and/or company. Unlike the job interview, the purpose is to get information only.

 Some people succeed by great talent, some by the influence of friends, some by a miracle. But the majority succeed by hard work.
— Eleanor Roosevelt

Phone a person who is in the occupation you are interested in or the head of a department you'd like to work in. State your purpose and ask for an appointment. If the person doesn't have time, ask for a telephone inter-  view. Make it clear that you are not applying for a job there and that you'll be brief, not more than five minutes. For more on informational interviewing, read Richard Bolles' *What Color Is Your Parachute?* (Ten Speed Press, 1985).

If you succeed in lining up an appointment, wear your best job hunting outfit. Have a list of questions ready so you won't waste the person's time. In fact, have the questions ready when you telephone in case the person agrees to answer them over the phone.

INFORMATION IN PRINT

NEWSPAPERS: National newspapers are an excellent source of up-to-date information on industries and major companies; the local newspaper is best for information on local economic conditions and small, local companies. News articles, especially those in the business section, often give hot tips on companies and industries that are thriving and those which are having problems.

The major national newspapers have a daily, separate business section. They also issue a yearly supplement on the labor market outlook and overall national and regional economies. It's a good idea to read what's in store for the region you hope to work in.

Do your own "market research" on local job market conditions and pay scales. A simple tally of advertised job openings will give you a general picture of occupations and companies that are thriving as well as the salary range for your occupation. You may also discover job opportunities you hadn't even considered.

MAGAZINES, JOURNALS AND NEWSLETTERS: Magazines which focus on business, labor and general economic conditions include *Business Week, Fortune, MONEY, Forbes Magazine.* Others which focus on specific industries and technologies are excellent sources of specialized information (e.g., *INFOWORLD, High Technology, Journal of Marketing, Human Resources Management, Telecommunications*).

STOCK MARKET TRENDS: Study the company's stock price trends in the financial pages. Visit the local stock brokerage office. Ask for research reports on the company and its current annual reports, manuals and brochures. If you detect financial problems, you'll know it's going to be difficult to find a job there. A rise in stock price is an indication the company is doing well and may be expanding. This means more employees may be hired.

Read the *Value Line Investment Survey* which gives information for investors on over 1,600 companies. Read business magazines, *The Wall Street Journal* and the business section of national newspapers to learn how the industry as a whole is doing.

TRADE AND PROFESSIONAL NEWSLETTERS AND JOURNALS generally contain more up-to-date information about jobs, employers and industries than books. Some have classified ads that list a wide range of job openings in the industry and their salaries.

COMPANY MANUALS describe the firm's major business activities and its divisions and branches. Names, addresses and phone numbers of key persons to contact are included. Various occupations within the firm may be described, together with their training, education and skills requirements. There may also be instructions on how to apply for a job with the company. The manuals give an insider's look at the firm and what it's like to be an employee.

40

ANNUAL REPORTS by major companies generally give a rosy view of their activities in order to encourage investors. But they usually list the names of directors and officers, address of corporate headquarters and the number of employees.

An annual report may describe the pension plan; operations and products or services; functions and location of plants, branches and subsidiaries; acquisitions; and future plans.

The full financial status of the current year is compared with those of the previous 5 to 10 years so you can see at a glance how the company has progressed. Also included are the sources and use of working capital and earnings per share of dividends.

You may also find a report on current problems such as lawsuits and civil actions against the company, losses incurred by unprofitable operations, and more.

You may be able to get a copy by phoning the company. If not, try the library or the local brokerage office.

ANNUAL BUDGET: According to Elizabeth Fowler (*The New York Times* "Careers" column), new positions are generally created when a company prepares its annual budget. These are usually prepared on a calendar year basis. Therefore, January is the best time for management and professional level people to be hired.

Phone the companies for these reports or see if the library has them.

CURRENT BOOKS: The authors of the books described in the Appendix have done much of the slave work for you. They have:

Inside information on selected, major companies which would take you many months to find on your own.

Additional criteria you can use to assess a company which is not included in the book.

They may also give you ideas on questions to ask at the interview.

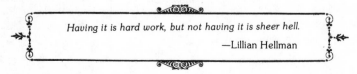

Having it is hard work, but not having it is sheer hell.

—Lillian Hellman

THE "BIG GUY"

THE "THINK TANK"

THE "NERVE CENTER"

Desks made of oak are at the bottom,
and those of walnut are next.
Then, moving up,
mahogany is . . . "upper middle class,"
until we arrive at the apex: teak.

In the army, at ladies' social
functions, pouring the coffee is the
prerogative of the senior officer's wife
because, as the ladies all know,
coffee outranks tea.
—"Class" by Paul Fussell (Summit Books)

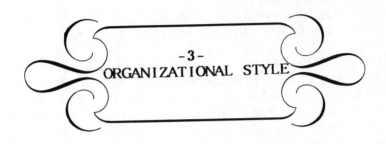

-3-
ORGANIZATIONAL STYLE

re you and the organization compatible? Organizations have "personality" and a set of values and beliefs, just as you do. They vary in their goals and style of achieving them, in their decision-making structure, pace of innovation, and code of behavior.

Ideally, all employees of an organization, from the top executive to the least skilled workers, share its beliefs, values and basic style. When this is not so, the following real life events can occur.

Middle aged worker, fired because he couldn't adapt to changes in worker-management relations, files age discrimination suit and loses.

Several executives are persuaded to leave Fortune 500 corporations to head high-tech firms. Within a year they fail miserably. The reason? Their style and that of the firms clash head on. "He came from old-line business and really belonged there. He was too authoritarian... and we don't have kings here," said a high-tech official of a dismissed executive.

AN ORGANIZATION'S STYLE GENERALLY REFLECTS THE PERSONALITY OF ITS FOUN-

43

DER AND/OR CURRENT LEADER. It's also shaped by the standards shared by most companies in a particular industry as the following expressions illustrate:

Banker sobriety
Wall Street propriety
Pin stripe personality
Organization man/woman
Buttoned-down (name of company)
Hard hat (construction, heavy manufacturing)

"CONSERVATIVE," "HIERARCHICAL," "TRATIONAL," "BUREAUCRATIC," AND "AUTHORITARIAN" are terms that have been used to describe organizations in the old-line industries (i.e., insurance, banking, oil, finance, government, heavy manufacturing, public education, health care). They are called "old-wave" or "sunset" industries because their style of doing things is being challenged by the "sunrise" or "new-wave" industries of science and high technology.

Companies in this category tend to have a management style in which orders issued from above go down the line and are expected to be carried out to the letter. Some have a chain of command that is as strict as the army's. There is a sense of security in knowing exactly what your responsibilities are, but you'll have less freedom to decide how to carry them out or question directives.

OLD-WAVE" ORGANIZATIONS TEND TO HAVE THE FOLLOWING CHARACTERISTICS, according to various studies and newspaper reports:

Strong leadership
Clear lines of authority
Older top level people (45-plus)
Conservative dress code enforced
Cautious employees rewarded; risk takers frowned on
Position and titles emphasized; fear/respect relationship between superiors and subordinates
Less open to change and innovation (because they have too much invested in older technology)

 The past went that-a-way. — Marshall McLuhan

Climb up the ladder slow and limited

Prefer to hire people who have personality traits similar to those of top executives; who are comfortable (or willing) to follow the leader in every way. (If the chief executive officer drinks blond Dubonnets, everyone drinks blond Dubonnets.)

Uniformity of personality preferred for speedier decision making and fulfillment of orders (unlike high-tech firms which view their workers as individualists and accept "doing your own thing" as long as it raises the bottom line.)

If you are ambitious and in a hurry, casual and informal, creative, a risk taker, an independent thinker, one who works best in times of crisis--this type of organization will drive you up the wall.

INDICATORS OF THE OLD-WAVE ORGANIZATION include:

Time clocks

Strict dress code

Orderly, steady work pace

Relatively quiet work setting

No long-haired or bearded male employees

Women employees wear the male equivalent of the gray flannel suit.

Preference for hierarchy and rules (Communications go down the line, from top to bottom. These are generally in written form, with many copies.)

Executive offices are elegant (rare oil paintings, jacuzzis, the works), depending on the disposable wealth of the organization. Used as a display of the power, prestige and wealth of the organization.

Floor plans and offices are designed so that top management and lower level workers rarely meet face-to-face. Executives may enjoy reserved parking and separate dining quarters, entrances and washrooms.

NEW-WAVE, SUNRISE COMPANIES: Generally, decisions are made on the basis of consensus among many or all levels of employees. Workers have more freedom to decide how and when to carry out their assignments. A major purpose is to foster an entrepreneurial spirit. Some labor experts predict this man-

style is the wave of the future in the U.S.
il class" distinctions between management and
white and blue collar workers are muted or non-
They all work together, eat together and play
together. Workers share in decisions traditionally made
by management. They may decide on, for example:

Work hours
Quality standards
Work organization
Department budgets
Discipline measures
Production schedules

Apple Computer, Inc. is a model sunrise company. It
was started in a garage by a 22-year old college dropout, Steven Jobs, who became chairman of the board, and
a kid electronics genius, Stephen Wozniak. It is said
that at Apple you can't tell the difference between "so-
called" management and employees. Apple prides itself in
being known as an innovative company.

In new-wave companies, loyalty is defined as including creativity and innovation. The old fashioned defi-
nition included rigid conformity to rules (such as the
dress code) and blindly following orders year after
year, often staying with the same company 20 or more
years. Today, such an employee is increasingly viewed as
"dull, dependent and a drag on corporate dynamism."

SIGNS INDICATING A SUNRISE, NEW-WAVE
ORGANIZATION:

Noisier atmosphere
Tight, frequent deadlines
No-frills executive offices
Fast paced, highly charged work environment
Young top management (Apple's Chairman of the Board,
Steven Jobs, was 29 in 1984.)
Young employees (In 1984, the average age of Apple
employees was 29.)
Workers generally willing to put in long workdays. A

 In an era of fierce foreign competition and rapid technological change, the person who is averse to taking risks, who requires structure, who refrains from expressing himself for fear of jeopardizing his job and who follows corporate policies even if they lead to disaster (is obsolete).
—Jeanne D. McDowell

46

T-shirt worn in Silicon Valley, California, reads "I work 90 hours a week and am proud of it.")

Few strict rules ("Doing your own thing" is encouraged as long as it raises the bottom line.)

Casual clothes, even jeans, sneakers and sports shirts (An old-line executive hired by a high tech company describes the sort of culture clash that can occur. He arrived at his boss's home for a party wearing a jacket and tie. All the other guests were in beach attire.)

More direct lines of communication between managers and employees (The same executive reports his amazement at a meeting in which the president's distribution plan was hooted down by subordinate employees.)

Common dining quarters (At Syntex Corporation in Palo Alto, California, the president eats breakfast each morning in the employee cafeteria.)

Egalitarian floor plan and offices designed so that top level employees and workers meet on common ground (same elevators, hallways, washrooms, parking space, entrances, dining rooms.)

Frequent after-hours get-togethers and parties, some very elaborate (This is in keeping with the goal of creating and maintaining a total "family" work environment and also to keep highly skilled workers happy so they won't leave.)

SMALL BUSINESSES SHARE MANY CHARACTERISTICS OF LARGE COMPANIES IN THE NEW-WAVE INDUSTRIES. For example, entrepreneurship and creativity are encouraged.

The personal qualities preferred by employers (see chapter one) are even more critical because there is more togetherness and informality than in large, bureaucratic organizations.

Also, someone who won't pull his own weight has no place to hide. While there is more opportunity to do and learn in a small business, everyone is expected to pitch in, regardless of job title. It's no place for the person who doesn't like to do the grimy, unpleasant work that comes up from time to time.

If you appear too concerned about job security and benefits (i.e., life insurance and pension plans), you'll give the impression of being more suitable for the old-wave style than the risk-taking, entrepreneurial style of a small business.

IT WOULD BE A MISTAKE TO LUMP ALL THE COMPANIES IN AN INDUSTRY UNDER THE SAME LABEL. There are companies in the old-line industries which were experimenting with the new organizational style in 1985. These included General Motors, Citibank, AT&T, Dana, Honeywell, Jones & Laughlin, People Express, Proctor & Gamble and Westinghouse.

Even in a staid, conservative company there may be special job openings which call for a more independent, flamboyant style (e.g., a super-salesman; lobbyist to push a special project).

It depends on the owners. Some large companies (e.g., Wang Laboratories with over 35,000 employees in 1985) attempt to create the informal, innovative spirit of small companies. At McDonalds, there is even a title of vice-president for individuality.

THE REGION IN WHICH A COMPANY DIVISION OR BRANCH IS LOCATED ALSO INFLUENCES THE COMPANY STYLE. (e.g., the Southwest, California and New York each has its own distinctive "style" of American culture). Sears Roebuck & Co., although highly centralized, has divisions with their own distinctive brand of the parent style. Allstate, for example, is described as having a "midwestern" (more casual) style.

ALSO, KEEP IN MIND THAT THE "SUNRISE" TYPE IS A NEW PHENOMENON IN THIS COUNTRY. A 1984 survey of companies with more than 100 employees showed that only 14% had the new management style. Experts predict the number will rise as pressures from foreign competition and technological advances requiring new adaptations increase.

THE BEST WAY TO DETERMINE WHETHER A COMPANY FOLLOWS THE GENERAL, INDUSTRY PATTERN is to:
Read about it in the newspapers.
Get inside information from your personal contacts.
If it's clear the job offer is yours, ask the interviewer if you may meet or have lunch with the employees.
Check for tell-tale indicators listed above.
Ask the interviewer directly: "Can you tell me what it's like to work for this company?" or, "What management style does this company prefer?"

Over the next generation . . . society's greatest opportunities will lie in tapping human inclinations toward collaboration and compromise rather than . . . competition and rivalry.
—Derek C. Bok, President of Harvard University

-4-
BEHIND THE SCENES
OF
THE JOB INTERVIEW

THE INTERVIEW IS AN OPPORTUNITY TO GET DETAILED INFORMATION ABOUT THE JOB AND THE COMPANY WHICH WILL HELP YOU DECIDE IF THAT'S WHAT YOU REALLY WANT. Some applicants approach the interview as if they were entering a beauty contest. Each "contestant" displays his/her "assets" and the lucky winner is then chosen by a panel of judges.

Laura D, an honors college senior, was recruited by a Long Island accounting firm. She was so flattered that she accepted without question the interviewer's assurances there would be "just a little" overtime work and "occasional" travel into Manhattan.

As it turned out, the job involved 55 to 60 hours a week without extra pay. And, she spent more time commuting to accounts in Manhattan than in Long Island where she and her fiancee had bought a house they planned to renovate on weekends. With overtime work and mortgage payments due, it was impossible to look for a better job. She was stuck with a job she hated and an employer she resented for not leveling with her.

Laura should have taken a more active role in the interview instead of passively waiting to be "judged." She, too, had a right to ask questions. ("Can you be more specific about the amount of overtime?" "On the average, how often will I be working in Manhattan?" "Will this be in writing?")

FROM THE EMPLOYER'S POINT OF VIEW, the purpose of the interview is to learn more about you than the resume and cover letter reveal; to find out whether your abilities, interests, personality and appearance match the requirements of the job and the organization. The employer wants assurance that you'll be a happy, productive worker who won't quit at the earliest opportunity.

Hiring the wrong person can cost an employer thousands of dollars in lost time and productivity. New employees need more supervision and training. They're more likely to make mistakes, have accidents, and waste time and materials. A whole new round of advertising the job, and selecting and training a replacement doubles the cost. For a small company, a high turnover can make the difference between profit and loss for the year.

THE SELECTION PROCESS TYPICALLY STARTS WITH A REVIEW OF THE RESUME AND LETTER OF APPLICATION. A single job opening may bring in hundreds. Often there is barely time to scan each one. (That's why the resume should be brief, with the most important information on the first half of the first page.) Then the most promising applicants are invited to an interview. Hopefully, you are among these.

While you wait for the interview to begin, a secretary will give you an application form to fill out. After the interviewer examines the completed form, the interview begins.

FOR CERTAIN JOBS, YOU MAY BE INTERVIEWED BY MORE THAN ONE OFFICER OF THE ORGANIZATION. After this hurdle is passed, there may be a written and/or physical examination. It depends on the occupation and the employer.

Some civil service jobs, for example, require a minimum passing grade on a written exam before there is any interview. In large companies, a written examination is more likely to be administered after the interview.

NEXT, THE CREDENTIALS OF SUCCESSFUL CANDIDATES ARE USUALLY VERIFIED. Former employers, supervisors, teachers and professors may be contacted by letter or a phone call from the prospective employer.

Occasionally, a person is hired solely on the basis of the resume and interview. No attempt is made to contact former employers and other persons given as references, sometimes to the regret of a hapless employer.

Some employers may ask you to bring proof of your training and education. Some will ask you to declare, in writing, that the statements on your resume or job application form are true. (The fine print at the bottom of the application form states this as a legally binding affirmation.) Any lies uncovered later are justifiable cause for dismissal.

MORE EMPLOYERS ARE INVESTIGATING A JOB CANDIDATE'S PAST THESE DAYS. In fact, some hire investigating agencies to verify the credentials of applicants for jobs paying higher than average salary or jobs involving sensitive matters. Large companies are more likely to do this. Smaller companies are more likely to contact previous employers themselves.

This state of affairs has come about because of a recent increase in falsification. Social scientists attribute this to the severe competition for good jobs and a changed code of ethics. A sensational example is the case of the journalist who was hired on the basis of unverified credentials. She won the Pulitzer Prize for her articles on childhood drug addiction which turned out to be pure fiction, as was her educational background.

THE ITEMS MOST FREQUENTLY CHECKED are education and previous employment. Some employers also check credit history.

SOME EMPLOYERS ALSO LOOK INTO COURT AND ARREST RECORDS AND POSSIBLE ALCOHOL AND DRUG ABUSE. In 1985, due to a widespread increase in cocaine use, about 25% of the Fortune 500 companies required a urinalysis screening for job applicants at all levels. These tests can show positive results days and weeks after drug use. New York and other cities recently began screening for potential child molesters who apply for jobs at nursery schools.

Polygraph (lie detector) tests may be administered to determine if a candidate answers certain questions truthfully (e.g., criminal record, involvement in subversive activities). However, in 1985 more than 20 states had a ban on the use of lie detectors in hiring procedures as an unwarranted invasion of privacy.

SOME JOB HUNTERS REASSURE A PROSPECTIVE EMPLOYER BY PAYING A FEE TO AN INVESTIGATING AGENCY. The National Credential Verification Service in Minneapolis, 12247 Nicollet Ave. S, Burnsville (612/894-3950), for example, verifies the job seeker's credentials and issues a card which can be presented at the interview. The card lists the phone number of the agency which the employer calls in order to verify that what is on the resume is true.

THE INTERVIEW GETS POOR GRADES AS A VALID AND RELIABLE MEANS OF SELECTING THE BEST POSSIBLE PERSON FOR THE

JOB. Yet, most employers still rely on it as the sole basis for hiring decisions. As you read the following, you'll see why it's silly to be down on yourself when you get a "We are sorry to inform you..." letter.

OFTEN, CRITERIA THAT HAVE NO ABILITY TO PREDICT WORK PERFORMANCE ARE INVOLVED IN HIRING DECISIONS (e.g., sex, age, race, outfit worn, attitudes).

EYE CONTACT is another frequently mentioned factor. One psychological study found that interviewers who had made an "accept" decision often said, "Eye contact was good." Conversely, those who decided to reject an applicant mentioned, "Poor eye contact" as one of the reasons.

PHYSICAL APPEARANCE CAN BE THE DECIDING FACTOR. That's why it's important to follow appropriate dress and grooming standards.

INTERVIEWERS OFTEN FORM AN IMPRESSION OF AN APPLICANT'S PERSONALITY AND USE THIS AS A BASIS FOR JUDGING JOB QUALIFICATIONS. The "halo effect" is at work when an applicant is judged as all good or all bad on the basis of just one trait. It may be something totally irrelevant to the job, such as the color coordination of the outfit worn.

ATTITUDES AND BELIEFS THAT ARE SIMILAR TO THE INTERVIEWER'S CAN HELP. Psychological studies show these do influence hiring decisions. However, there is disagreement on the strength of this influence. Some studies show a stronger influence on the amount of salary offered. Applicants whose views differed substantially were offered a much lower salary, thereby discouraging them from accepting the job.

A reason for dressing like the chief executive officers, for accepting their values and beliefs as one's own (or pretending to) is that employers generally hire and promote those who resemble them most. They don't do this consciously. Sociological studies show this to be the case in other areas of life as well.

ATTITUDES AND INTERESTS CAN BE OBTAINED FROM THE INTERVIEW, JOB APPLICATION FORM AND RESUME. A simple conversational topic or a seemingly innocuous question can be used to elicit attitudes, beliefs and overall compatibility with the job and the company. For example, after a series of direct, factual questions, the interviewer relaxes and says, "So, you visited San Francisco? I have a nephew who lives there. What do you think of it?" (San Francisco has a large gay population. Steer clear of this topic.)

THE MORE YOU HAVE IN COMMON WITH THE INTERVIEWER, THE BETTER. Any shared experience or interest which establishes rapport is a plus. For example, you both:

Have mutual acquaintances.
Worked for the same company.
Lived in the same community.
Graduated from the same school.
Share the same leisure interests.
Vacation in the same tourist area.
Belong to the same special interest group.

A FINAL DECISION IS INFLUENCED MORE BY NEGATIVE THAN BY POSITIVE INFORMATION A reject decision is generally reached fairly early in the interview; experienced interviewers take an average of less than four minutes! The earlier the negative information comes up, the earlier the decision.

With highly qualified applicants, the decision usually takes longer, as long as ninety

minutes. The deciding factors generally occur late in the interview.

Some interviewers appear unusually harsh because they start out by deliberately seeking negative information. Once this phase is over, they soften up.

PLAY IT SAFE! DON'T REVEAL YOUR OPINIONS, LIKES AND DISLIKES ON TOUCHY TOPICS.

Religion	Affirmative action
Sex	Single parenthood
Race relations	Politics
Social policies	Abortion

Stick to safe topics, such as sports, vacation areas and weather. Better yet, mention interests and activities which show that you are compatible with the job and the company. (e.g., A pinball player or a motorcycle club member is unlikely to fit in with a golf or country club set.)

THE INTERVIEW IS BASED ON THE ASSUMPTION THAT JOB APPLICANTS ARE AND DO AS THEY SAY. Interviewers are aware there is a high possibility of faking the answers to some questions. (However, if hired and later found out, lying can lead to a dismissal.

MANY SMALL BUSINESS OWNERS DON'T HAVE JOB DESCRIPTIONS. They don't have a clear idea of what specific responsibilities are involved and the education and training needed. Often, they ask for more education than the job requires. Therefore, it's easier to convince a small business employer that you are right for the job.

YOUR FATE MAY DEPEND ON WHETHER YOU COME FIRST, IN THE MIDDLE OR NEAR THE END OF A SERIES OF INTERVIEWS. Psychologists call this the "halo effect." It means that an average applicant who is interviewed after several "lemons" will shine by comparison. Studies show the halo effect can account for as much as 80% of the shift up or down the rating scale.

If your qualifications are about average, you stand a better chance of getting a favorable rating if you are among the last to be interviewed.

CAUTION: If you wait too long to apply for the job, it may be too late.

However, if your qualifications are excellent, it doesn't matter at what point you are interviewed.

INTERVIEWERS GENERALLY PAY LEAST ATTENTION TO INFORMATION THAT COMES IN THE MIDDLE OF THE INTERVIEW. THEY PAY MOST ATTENTION TO WHAT COMES TOWARD THE BEGINNING AND END. Therefore, your chances of getting a good rating increase if you bring up favorable information about yourself near the end or beginning of the interview.

Conversely, your chances of getting a poor rating increase if negative information comes up near the end or beginning of the interview. (If it comes up in the mid-point, it's more likely to be forgotten or overlooked.)

The exception occurs where a tentative decision has already been made on the basis of information the interviewer receives about you before the interview. In this case, any positive or negative information presented early in the interview has the greatest influence on the final decision.

THE QUALITY OF THE INTERVIEW DEPENDS ON THE SKILL AND JUDGMENT OF THE PERSON WHO INTERVIEWS YOU. A typical interview places a superhuman burden on the interviewer's ability to extract information from you that is not on the resume and then evaluate your compatibility with the job and the organization. All this has to be decided within 10 to 20 minutes. After you have gone, all this information must be recalled accurately and a final decision made.

THAT'S WHY IT'S IMPORTANT TO SEND A FOLLOW-UP LETTER AND/OR A MINI-RESUME which highlights all the important points covered in the interview. Do this as soon as you get home so the interviewer has a chance to see it before a hiring decision is made.

THERE IS NO SUCH THING AS A STANDARD INTERVIEW. This makes your chances of being hired even more dependent on who interviews you. Studies show that interviewers seldom ask the same questions of different applicants. Even when they ask the same question, they often disagree on the appropriateness of an applicant's response.

Information that is considered important by one interviewer may be totally ignored by another. Studies reveal there is often disagreement on the relative importance of appearance, social skills, health, outside interests, marital status, number of children and, yes, even education!

SOME EMPLOYERS USE AN EVALUATION FORM AS A WAY OF REDUCING THE EFFECTS OF BIAS AND SUBJECTIVITY. It may include hundreds of specific criteria which the interviewer rates on a positive to negative scale. For example,

Teamwork	Initiative
Job Skills	Creativity
Credibility	Appearance
Intelligence	Punctuality
Social Skills	Flexibility
School Grades	Personality
Meets Deadlines	Self-presentation
Outside Interests	Need For Supervision
Job Related Knowledge	Prior Work Experience
Communications Skills	

YOUR PERSONALITY AND THE WAY YOU DESCRIBE YOURSELF CAN HAVE FAR MORE EFFECT ON THE HIRING DECISION THAN YOUR WORK EXPERIENCE. According to studies, the "Scout virtues" will get you to first base in almost all occupations. If you also have the desired job qualifications, you're almost certain to get the job.

Don't be humble. You're not that great.

— Golda Meir

AN APPLICANT WHO IS VIEWED AS "WARM" IS RATED SIGNIFICANTLY HIGHER THAN ONE WHO IS "RATHER COLD." That's why eye contact, facial expressiveness and a smile are so important.

APPLICANTS WHO EXHIBIT THE FOLLOWING TRAITS GET A LOW RATING.
"Too passive"
"Lacks self-confidence"
"Doesn't like people"

HUMILITY AND MODESTY WON'T GET YOU TO FIRST BASE IN A JOB INTERVIEW. It's important to describe yourself favorably. Studies show that applicants who have a high opinion of themselves, and make this explicit, are given higher ratings. If you have a self-deprecating manner, it doesn't matter how many of the desired personality traits you possess. The interviewer will see you as you see yourself.

IF YOUR SELF-DESCRIPTION FITS THE INTERVIEWER'S GENERAL IDEA OF THE TYPE OF PERSONALITY WHICH FITS THE JOB, THERE'S A GOOD POSSIBILITY YOU WILL GET IT. Studies show that measures of personality traits accurately predict how well a person will do on the job. The way you describe yourself is one "measure."

Interviewers are more likely to overlook deficiencies in your other qualifications if your personality is compatible with the job and the company "personality."

DO YOUR HOMEWORK. LEARN ALL YOU CAN ABOUT THE JOB AND THE PERSONALITY TRAITS IT REQUIRES. Personality traits that ensure a happy marriage with one occupation can lead to divorce with another. Jobs that involve influencing, dealing with, manipulating, and educating people

60

require a different set of personality traits than jobs that involve working with ideas, numbers, animals or plants.

Example: Jobs that involve recruiting, supervising, selling, fund raising and other tasks which require influencing people need workers with the following characteristics:

Well organized	Communications skills
Doesn't give up easily	Ambitious
Optimistic	Dominant personality
Enjoys the limelight	Likes to plan in detail
Enjoys being with people	

An applicant who displays the following traits won't get the job, even though he/she is a genius, a Harvard Ph.D. and is absolutely gorgeous.

Inarticulate	Impulsive
Moody, depressed	Carefree
Lacks self-confidence	Gives up easily
Introverted	A loner
Enjoys solving abstract problems	

Example: Human service jobs (e.g., nurse, social worker, counselor, teacher) demand a high degree of the following traits:

"Scout" virtues	Gregarious
Likable	Likes to help
Human relations skills	Warm, outgoing
Doesn't give up easily	Communications skills

"TELL ME ABOUT YOURSELF." Certain questions are asked in order to reveal more about your personality and how well it fits the job and the company. Here is an excerpt from a study done on impressions of personality in the job interview. It illustrates an applicant for a counseling job whose self-description gets a high rating.[1]

INTERVIEWER: *"Could you tell me a little more about yourself, your interests and so on?"*

APPLICANT: *"I feel worthwhile when I'm*

helping someone who is disabled. Seeing old or helpless people makes me feel I would like to take care of them—help them...People tell me their troubles because they know I'll help them...I'm quite effective in getting others to agree with me. I feel confident directing other people's activities...I'm never one to sit on the sidelines at a party. I enjoy entertaining others. They think I'm lively and witty...."

FOR CERTAIN JOBS IT'S MORE IMPORTANT TO DESCRIBE ONE'S TECHNICAL, INTEL-LECTUAL AND/OR PROFESSIONAL INTERESTS AND COMPETENCE. Personality plays a far less significant role in jobs like statistician, engineer, scientist, accountant, interior decorator. It's best to describe outside activities and interests which highlight the abilities and interests which match the job.

For example, a person applying for a job as computer programmer would describe interests which indicate a problem solving, logical and analytic mind as well as attention to detail and organization:

Solving crossword puzzles	Reading mystery stories
Solving math problems	Collecting coins
Composing music	Dress pattern making

YOUR ABILITY TO HANDLE STRESS MAY BE ASSESSED AT THE INTERVIEW. This is likely to happen if the job involves a lot of stress, such as many deadlines or dealing with the public.

No sane interviewer is going to ask you outright, "Are you calm when under stress?" The only way to find out is to ask indirect questions. These have no wrong or right answers and may even seem far-fetched.

Another tactic is to arrange for mildly stressful events to occur during the interview in order to see how you react. There may be frequent, annoying interruptions such as doors slamming and phones ringing. The applicant may be bombarded by nonstop questions fired at him/her by as many as ten people. Nearly 10% of executives looking for top international jobs walk out in the middle of interviews which are too stressful, reports England's Executive Employment Bulletin.

The way to deal with this is to know in advance that such situations might occur so you won't be taken by surprise.

"Before going to the interview, say to yourself, 'If I can't handle the stress involved I should honestly ask myself whether I can handle the day to day pressures of the job,'" advises Josephine Lerro, former director of human resources at TempsAmerica. "The interviewer will be asked to bombard the candidate in order to test his/her poise; so maybe the candidate who worries about it should not be there to begin with."

Don't take what appear to be hostile questions personally. Remind yourself that the interviewer is trying to do his/her job and holds no personal grudge against you.

Don't be too shy to ask, "Will you please tell me why this information is so important to you?"

ℐNTERVIEWS DIFFER IN THE FOLLOWING WAYS, depending on the type of job opening and the applicant's qualifications:

    1. DURATION OF INTERVIEW: A single interview can be as brief as 10 minutes or as long as 7 hours.

    2. THE NUMBER OF TIMES AN APPLICANT IS INTERVIEWED: Generally, a single interview is all that's needed for jobs below the mana-

gement and professional level.

Two or more interviews may be required if the job demands professional, managerial and high level technical skills or if it involves much stress (as in dealing with many  deadlines or a demanding public), and where the employee represents the organization's public interest.

Furthermore, as more companies switch to decision making which involves workers at all levels, more attention will be paid to certain personality factors (teamwork, adaptability cooperation) and communications skills. Several interviews may be required to weed out unsuitable candidates.

If you're called back for a second or third interview, it means you are being seriously considered for the job.

3. THE NUMBER OF INTERVIEWERS ALSO VARIES ACCORDING TO THE JOB. The more complex abilities and knowledge that are required, the more sensitive the job responsibilities (e.g., defense matters), the more likely you'll find several interviewers firing questions at you.

APPLICANTS MAY BE ASKED TO DEMONSTRATE THEIR ABILITIES FOR JOBS INVOLVING COMPLEX SKILLS AND KNOWLEDGE. You may be asked to do some typing or word processing, repair some equipment or explain how you would solve a problem.

A candidate for a management level job might be asked, "How would you handle this situation? A valued worker is having marital problems and is drinking heavily. His work productivity is slacking off and he's often absent from work on Fridays or Mondays." or "Someone in your department is spreading malicious rumors and it's hurting morale. What would you do?"

SOME PERSONNEL DEPARTMENTS ADMINISTER TESTS to assess personality, reading comprehension, manual dexterity, spatial ability and/or numerical and verbal problem solving ability.

Generally, it's the large companies which administer

64

such tests. Some job placement agencies also administer tests in order to assure employers that the persons they recommend possess the required abilities. Many government jobs require a minimum passing grade on civil service exams.

Hiring decisions are not based on test scores alone. Other factors are taken into account, and often these carry more weight. If an applicant's other qualifications are good, a below average score is often disregarded. Recruiters know that a single test score is an insufficient measure of a person's suitability for a job.

APTITUDE AND SKILLS TESTS are relatively easy for most people. They assess basic skills in spelling and vocabulary, reading comprehension, arithmetic and mathematics, reasoning, and the ability to follow directions. (That's why it's important for you to read the job application form carefully and to answer the questions completely and clearly.)

These are multiple choice tests. You don't even have to write out your answers. All that's needed is to mark the right answer among a given set of answers. The score is based on the number of correct choices you make in a given period of time.

In a reading comprehension test, for example, all you have to do is read several short paragraphs and then mark the correct answer from among four or five given answers. Its purpose is to assess how well you understand what you have read. The numerical reasoning tests estimate your ability to apply what you learned in elementary and high school to solve simple, everyday problems.

TAKING TIMED, MULTIPLE CHOICE TESTS IS A SKILL THAT IS EASILY LEARNED. One of the skills is knowing how to optimize the correct number of choices you make in the allotted time.

It's important to listen carefully to the instructions given before the test begins. If there is something you don't understand, ask questions no matter how stupid or trivial they seem to you. If you wait until after the test starts, you will lose valuable seconds which can lower your score.

Every second counts in a timed test. Have everything you might need on hand so you can work steadily and not waste time rummaging in your handbag or briefcase, for handkerchief, chewing gum, eraser, etc.

Don't waste time pondering over diffi-  cult questions. Answer all the easy ones first. Skip over the difficult ones, mar- king these lightly so that when you're ready to go back to them, you'll waste no time finding them.

IF POSSIBLE, LEARN IN ADVANCE IF THE JOB REQUIRES TAKING A TEST. Phone the personnel department or read about the occupation in the *Occupational Outlook Handbook.* If it's a civil service job, contact your state Job Service office.

BE SMART AND PREPARE IN ADVANCE. The tests aren't difficult, but some people, especially older applicants who haven't taken a test in years, suffer from test anxiety. Borrow a stopwatch and prac- tice speeding up your rate of response to a few tests.

You can find sample tests to practice on in the public library and in school or college career guidance offices. Also, see if the local bookstore has the Arco series on tests for every conceivable occupation imagi- nable, including civil service jobs. The best way to get rid of test anxiety is to practice taking them in a stress-free situation.

"TELL ME ABOUT YOURSELF!"

𝒜 self-assessment involves analyzing your natural aptitudes and learned skills, your likes and dislikes, and other job-related aspects of your personality.

SIX GOOD REASONS FOR DOING A SELF-ASSESSMENT:

1. YOU'LL KNOW WHETHER THE CAREER YOU HAVE CHOSEN IS THE RIGHT ONE.
People often choose an occupation for the wrong reasons: family pressure, it seems "glamorous," their friends are in it, or they "fell" into it.

Often they have the skimpiest knowledge of what the occupation is all about and its future prospects. Then, one day, they discover they are square pegs in a round hole of a job. So, they remain dissatisfied, low-achieving employees or they periodically look for a "better" job.

2. YOU'LL BE ABLE TO CONVINCE AN EMPLOYER THAT YOU ARE THE BEST PERSON FOR THE JOB.

3. YOU'LL KNOW WHICH TYPE OF ORGANIZATION YOU'RE MOST COMPATIBLE WITH.
If you're asked, "Tell me about yourself," you'll be able to show that in addition to job compatibility, you and the organization are meant for each other.

4. YOU'LL BE ABLE TO CONVINCE THE EMPLOYER OF YOUR SUITABILITY FOR OTHER, RELATED JOB OPENINGS
if you are not offered the job (or, if you are asked, "Where do you see yourself in this company five years from now?") Employers can't hire every good applicant who applies for a single job opening. Often, they keep the resumes of promising persons for as long as a year in case another, suitable opening occurs.

5. IT WILL BE OBVIOUS TO THE EMPLOYER THAT YOU ARE SERIOUS ABOUT YOUR CAREER.
Employers see too many indifferent applicants who give irrelevant, hazy answers such as these:

"Where do you think you fit in our company?" [Hazy Answer: "Oh, I can do anything which involves people. I love working with people."]

"What would you like to be doing in five years?" [Naive Answer: "I'd like to be chief executive officer. I'm pretty good at planning and managing people. I was captain of my high school football team."]

6. YOU'LL HAVE THE FACTS TO SUPPORT YOUR CLAIM THAT YOU ARE WORTH MORE TO THE EMPLOYER THAN THE SALARY OFFERED.
(Or, you'll be able to negotiate a better benefits package.)

HOW TO DO A SELF-ASSESSMENT:
First, throw all modesty to the wind and take stock of your assets: the skills and knowledge you have acquired in a lifetime and your natural aptitudes.

> Anything that creates tension and causes you to ask, "Where am I going? What do I want?" is all to the good. Anxiety precedes periods of growth, transformation and development.
> — Dr. Michele Berdy, Clinical Psychologist

Next, learn which occupations and work environments match these assets.

Then, determine whether your skills and/or knowledge need updating. If they do, enroll in an adult education course. Only after you've done this will you be ready to tackle the interview.

Some people need the advice of an experienced career counselor to do a self-assessment. Some can do it themselves with the help of a guide book on the subject. Others have an idea of what they want but need a little hand-holding from the exercises below.

Whether you are a recent graduate, a homemaker looking for a better job after years of raising a family, or a worker displaced by technological change, you possess a unique set of assets which can be put to use in more ways than you think.

No matter how little formal education you've had, or how long ago you held a paid job, you have accumulated a valuable storehouse of skills, knowledge and experience which can be applied to several occupations, not just one. Especially in lean times, a job seeker who keeps as many options open as possible is better off than the narrow specialist with lots of degrees.

DOING A SELF-ASSESSMENT IS LIKE DRAWING UP A BALANCE SHEET OF YOUR ASSETS AND LIABILITIES.

ASSETS refers to your interests, learned skills, natural aptitudes and your work-related achievements and experiences. A set of skills and aptitudes is something you can do as well as, or better than, most people.

LIABILITIES, in this case, refers to any need for further training or education and any restrictions on your career choices caused by health or family reasons.

YOU CAN IDENTIFY YOUR ASSETS BY SCRUTINIZING, ONE BY ONE, YOUR:
1. Education and training
2. Favorite leisure activities
3. Paid work experience
4. Non-paid, voluntary work experience

Generally, people do best what they enjoy doing most. The following exercises will help you identify the occupations and work settings you are most likely to enjoy. (You don't have to do every exercise.) They will also prepare you for the job application form, which asks for your hobbies and other interests. Employers want to know this because they have learned that workers who enjoy their job and work environment are more productive.

Use several sheets of paper for each section of this outline:

A. PAID WORK EXPERIENCE
   1. Job responsibilities
   2. Skills and aptitudes required
   3. What I liked most about it
   4. What I disliked about it

B. VOLUNTARY WORK EXPERIENCE
   1. Job responsibilities
   2. Skills and aptitudes required
   3. What I liked most about it
   4. What I disliked about it

C. EDUCATION AND TRAINING
D. FAVORITE INTERESTS AND LEISURE ACTIVITIES
E. JOBS I WOULD LIKE TO HAVE
F. PERSONAL FACTORS

PAID WORK EXPERIENCE, list all the paid jobs you've had, including part time and freelance work. Put them in reverse chronological order, starting with the most recent job and going back in time. Leave ample space under each to include:
   1. Job title
   2. Employers' name and address
   3. Supervisor's name
   4. Dates of starting and leaving each job
   5. Starting and final pay
   6. Major responsibilities
   7. Major achievements and contributions
   8. Skills and aptitudes required

9. Likes/Dislikes

UNDER "MAJOR ACHIEVEMENTS AND CON-
TRIBUTIONS," write down the
things you did which went
beyond the normal expectations for the job. Here are a
few examples:

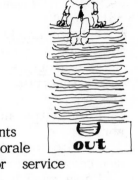

    Increased sales
    Decreased waste
    Saved employer money
    Saved hours of labor
    Increased space utilization
    Reduced number of customer complaints
    Increased office teamwork and/or morale
    Developed new procedure, product or service

DESCRIBE EACH ACHIEVEMENT IN DETAIL,
what you did and how you did it. For example, "I helped
reduce absenteeism in the office by substituting a flextime schedule for the old 9-to-5 routine. It was on an
experimental basis at first. Then, when attendance improved by 45% in the first quarter, it became permanent."

    Describe your achievements in measurable or other
specific descriptive terms wherever possible (hours,
dollars, percentages, quantity, quality). For example,
"My idea helped:

    - increase new orders by # percent."
    - increase monthly sales by # dollars."
    - lower costs by reducing # product defects."
    - reduce clerical errors by # percent."
    - simplify task difficulty by # percent."
    - improve the quality of our product (describe how)"
    - save # percent of office space for additional use."
    - reduce returned merchandise by # percent per
      month."
    - improve the delivery of service to our clients by #
      (hours/days/months)."
    - simplify the work flow with a savings of # (hours,
days,weeks) in production time."

✶✶✶

We have become a nation which seems to be blinded by scores.
— Red Barber

"SKILLS AND APTITUDES REQUIRED": Look over your list of responsibilities and achievements and ask yourself, "What assets do I possess which make me good at certain kinds of work?" Look also beyond the obvious ones, such as typing, filing, bookkeeping or selling. For example, are your strong points any of the following?

I <u>learn</u> <u>quickly</u>.

I <u>carry</u> <u>out</u> <u>orders</u> <u>quickly</u> <u>and</u> <u>accurately</u>.

I do <u>accurate</u> <u>detail</u> <u>work</u> and I enjoy it.

My supervisor has often said I'm good in <u>dealing</u> <u>with</u> <u>people</u>.

I'm <u>creative</u> in finding new and better ways to do my work.

I <u>write</u> <u>well</u>. The office manager has often complemented me on the letters I write.

I'm a <u>good</u> <u>leader</u>. (e.g., "People are generally willing to do as I say," "I was captain of my high school football team," "In my last job I was elected chairperson of the committee to ....", and so on.)

I'm a <u>fast</u> <u>worker</u>. I almost always meet deadlines, even if it meets giving up lunch hour or staying in after five.

I have <u>lots</u> <u>of</u> <u>energy</u>. You won't see me dragging around after 4:00 p.m. In the mornings, I don't need as much warm up time as some other workers do.

I'm <u>well</u> <u>organized</u>. I like to plan every detail of the work I must do. I don't plunge in without thinking carefully about it.

I'm good at <u>solving</u> <u>problems</u>. When the boss asks us for suggestions on how to lure more customers into the store, I generally have more ideas than most other workers.

Write down every single asset your work experience supports. Here is a list of action words o help you get started. Add others which apply especially to you. The nice thing about this exercise is that you can identify such abilities yourself, whether they were acquired in your life experience or through paid work.

 My daddy said to me, "Honey, if the Lord meant for you to work, he'd have given you skills."
          —Lynn von Furstenburg, socialite

Public speaking	Interviewing	Supervising
Cataloging	Budgeting	Directing
Mediating	Scheduling	Purchasing
Analyzing	Motivating	Organizing
Recruiting	Appraising	Screening
Negotiating	Lobbying	Repairing
Selling	Programming	Team work
Teaching	Fund raising	Hosting

Next, go through your list and check those words which express what you can do especially well.

Then, go over it again with a different color pencil and check those words which express what you enjoy doing most.

Finally, match these words with the appropriate work experiences that illustrate what you mean. For example, instead of saying, "I'm good at motivating workers under my supervision to do their best," you'll be able to cite specific examples of how you actually accomplished this and the amount of improved productivity.

Next, ask yourself, "What else did I do and learn that I can use in another position?" For example,

✱ DID YOU LEARN TO OPERATE A MACHINE? Sewing, industrial, robot, automobile, drill press, centrifuge, X-ray

✱ DID YOU LEARN TO USE OFFICE EQUIPMENT? Paper copier, overhead projector, calculator, word processor, laser printer, electronic typewriter, computer

✱ DID YOU LEARN A SPECIAL SKILL? Read maps, blueprints and charts; draw charts and graphs; program a computer; understand software manuals

List everything you learned which is related to the world of work, no matter how trivial it seems to you. You'd be surprised at the number of people who don't know how to use, for example, a paper copier or a typewriter. Typing skills are necessary for most employees these days, including managers and executives. This is because modern communications and electronic equipment is controlled by a typewriter-like keyboard.

Employers value such expertise because it saves them the time and money needed to train a new worker. It also shows you're not afraid of complicated, new equipment.

Let's suppose you've been a real estate salesperson and you are changing careers. First, you would identify every single task and responsibility you had in this occupation. Next, you would analyze each in detail. Each involves one or more skills and areas of knowledge The following is a list of some of the skills and expertise required in selling real estate. As you can see, these and other skills not mentioned can be applied to other occupations as well.

Appraising: Estimating the market value of houses.

Selling: Dealing with prospects to close deals.

Office Operating: Organizing and maintaining accurate records, answering phone inquiries.

Figuring: Estimating mortgage payments, interest rates.

Writing: Newspaper ads, sales notices and articles for real estate newsletter; composing letters to clients and members of real estate association.

Interviewing: Getting information from and about prospective tenants and landlords.

Reading Maps and Schematics: Studying district and road maps; blueprints.

Researching: Getting information from documents, census reports, survey data; making on-site observations of a neighborhood; interviewing for information.

Operating Equipment: Typing or word processing; operating a computer; using computer software; duplicating machine; driving a car; detecting defects in boilers, plumbing, etc.

"LIKES/DISLIKES": Write down aspects you especially liked and disliked about each job you've had. Put them under the following labels:

* Job Responsibilities
* Work Schedule: Night shift, overtime, deadlines, part time, etc.
* Physical Demands Of The Job: Standing, sitting, lifting heavy objects, peering into a microscope or computer screen, detailed eye-hand work, involves much traveling, etc.
* "Personality" Of The Organization: Conservative, bureaucratic, competitive, relaxed, fast paced, democratic, large, small, family owned, etc.
* Work Environment: Indoors-outdoors, city-suburbs, cramped-spacious, modern, own office-share office with others, transportation facilities, nearby cultural attractions.

Look over the list of likes and dislikes and number those aspects you would like to have in your next job in order of priority, from "Must have" to "Nice to have but not imperative."

Repeat the exercise under the heading, "What I don't want," again in order of priority.

FINALLY, STUDY YOUR LISTS. LOOK FOR THEMES WHICH RECUR THROUGHOUT ALL THE JOBS AND WORK SETTINGS. Here are some action words to get you started:

Writing
Planning
Researching
Detail work
Entertaining
Helping people
Public speaking
Keeping records
Solving problems
Working with ideas
Identifying problems
Working with hands
Working under pressure
Working indoors/outdoors

Applying numerical skills
Working alone/with others
Creating, inventing, designing
Carrying out other people's ideas
Working with plants, animals or objects
Exchanging information, ideas with others

NEXT, PICTURE YOURSELF IN THE IDEAL JOB and do a similar analysis. Then imagine the worst possible job in order to note the things you absolutely will not tolerate.

VOLUNTARY WORK EXPERIENCE: On a separate sheet of paper list all the non-paid work you have done, any active involvement in the community, school and other voluntary project. Include homemaking and child rearing responsibilities.

Do the same analysis as you did for "Paid Work Experience," using the same outline. The words on the skills lists for paid work also apply to nonpaid work.

Such voluntary responsibilities say something about the kind of person you are--your initiative, energy level, team spirit, intelligence, communications skills, social skills, creativity, leadership ability, organizing ability and ability to complete assignments and meet deadlines.

EMPLOYERS ARE ESPECIALLY INTERESTED IN THE FOLLOWING VOLUNTARY ACTIVITIES:
Hosted meeting
Prepared annual budget
Edited, wrote for newsletter
Designed, wrote advertising, flyers
Held office of president, treasurer...
Wrote articles, notices for newsletter
Organized conferences and other meetings
Raised funds (and met community leaders)

MANY WOMEN USE THE SKILLS DEVELOPED IN VOLUNTEER WORK TO GET PAID JOBS. Even entry level or part time work obtained as a result of volunteer work often leads to better paying, full time jobs.

Women's associations have had much success in helping women identify the skills acquired through non-paid work, and then negotiate these into paid jobs. Community colleges have special programs for women also. If you need such help, contact your local community college and/or one of the associations listed in the Appendix.

The following exercise illustrates some of the skills involved in volunteer activities. The purpose of this partial analysis is to show you how it's done.

Bear in mind that, of all the responsibilities a woman has had in volunteer work, employers value committee appointments and leadership positions the most. So, put these at the top of your list.

President/Chairperson: Organizing events; managing others; building, maintaining teamwork and morale

Fund Raising: Sales or persuading ability, planning and organizing fund drives, communications skills, knowledge of community resources, creative writing skills

Public Relations: Public speaking; planning, promoting, carrying out events; writing copy for the media; interviewing community leaders

Treasurer: Bookkeeping, purchasing for large gatherings, budgeting, preparing annual budget

Political Activities: Lobbying, research, public speaking, telephone interviewing

Preparing Newsletter: Writing; editing; layout, art and/or graphics work

Clerical: Keeping accurate, detailed reports; typing; writing letters, notices; organizing and filing documents; using office equipment

Hospital Work, Children's Camp: Counseling, teaching arts and crafts, nurse assistant

SKILLS WOMEN DEVELOP AS HOMEMAKERS WHICH ARE TRANSFERABLE TO PAID JOBS INCLUDE THE FOLLOWING:

Purchasing: Buying food, clothing, other family supplies

Financial: Budgeting family income; keeping a balance sheet on income and expenditures; income tax preparation; keeping track of debts, loan payments, mortgages, investments...

Clerical: Setting up files; keeping records; typing correspondence; proofreading and editing homework

Managing: Setting production goals (family plans), supervising, maintaining family morale and teamwork

Counseling: Spouse, neighbors, children, children's pals

Organizing, Planning: Seeing to it that family members get to school and work on time; maintaining steady flow of supplies for home; scheduling and coordinating a variety of activities, "personnel" and deadlines; maintaining order under pressure

Manual Dexterity: Any arts and crafts project, sewing, repair of small engines, carpentry, any other task requiring precise eye-brain-hand coordination

Office Equipment and Machinery You Learned To Use: Home computer, paper copier, printer, electronic typewriter, computer manuals, automobile, truck, VCR, word processor, camera

TRAINING AND EDUCATION

EDUCATION: Consider the knowledge and skills you learned in a formal setting such as high school, vocational or technical school, college, university and home study program.

TRAINING is what you learned in non-formal settings such as workshops, lectures, seminars and on-the-job. It is generally measured by actual performance. Even a one-day seminar or workshop should be included in your list if the topic is relevant to the job you want.

FIRST, CONSIDER ALL YOUR JOB-RELATED EDUCATION AND TRAINING. Don't forget to include evening and home study courses which increase your value to an employer. (Courses like "The Art of American Pie Baking" don't count.) Any self-improvement course, no matter how brief, should be included (e.g., public speaking, computer literacy, word processing).

NEXT, ASK YOURSELF THESE QUESTIONS:
- Which courses or training did I like best/least?
- In which did I do best?
- With which did I have most difficulty?

NOW, LIST ALL YOUR RELEVANT EXTRA-CURRICULAR ACTIVITIES. (Do this only if you were recently a student.) For example,

Class president
Discussion group leader
Editor of school newspaper
Member of school band, orchestra.
Planned, organized fund raising for the poor
A special interest club (Spanish, biology, photography, ...)

NEXT, THINK OF ALL THOSE SPECIAL EVENTS IN YOUR PAST WHICH SERVED AS CREATIVE LEARNING EXPERIENCES, WHICH RESULTED IN PERSONAL GROWTH. A good example of this is the case of an older woman who had hired a divorce lawyer recommended by a family friend, also an attorney. This "friend" then represented her husband. Not surprisingly, her attorney was too busy or unwilling to be of much help to her. This forced her to learn a few things on her own.

First, she learned how to use the law library. Then, step-by-step, she acquired other skills which eventually led to her becoming a self-taught expert in domestic law. With the help of a Displaced Homemaker Center, she was able to get on-the-job training which led to a paid job as legal paraprofessional. This provided the opportunity to establish a divorce clinic to help other women in similar circumstances.

INTERESTS AND LEISURE ACTIVITIES:
On a new sheet of paper list the interests and skills involved in your favorite leisure activities, those which are relevant to the job you want. Don't forget to include interests which you follow regularly in the newspapers, TV and magazines (e.g., stock market, photography, technology).

For example, if the job requires a high degree of eye-hand motor coordination, patience and concentration, you might mention leisure interests which also require these abilities (e.g., model airplane construction, crocheting, sewing.) Here are more examples of activities which involve occupational interests and abilities.

> Team sports
> Computer club
> Sketching, painting
> Learning foreign languages
> Writing short stories, poems
> Member of electronic bulletin board
> Creating computer programs in FORTRAN
> Repairing cars or small office equipment
> Little theater group (good for sales jobs)

NEXT, DO THE SAME TYPE OF ANALYSIS YOU DID WITH YOUR PREVIOUS LISTS.

FINALLY, REVIEW ALL YOUR LISTS AND LOOK FOR RECURRING THEMES OR PATTERNS.
Assuming there has been some consistency in your life experiences, the same themes will occur in your paid and volunteer work, education, training, leisure activities and interests. Ideally, these will match the requirements of the job you want. If not, now is the time to choose a career which will be a joy instead of just a job.

PERSONAL FACTORS: On this new page, evaluate your:
♥ ENERGY LEVEL: It should match the demands of the job and the pace of the company. Some companies, such as those in high technology, advertising

and the media, are fast paced and have frequent dead-lines. Will you be able to handle it?

♥ PHYSICAL LIMITATIONS should also be taken into account. Does the job involve more walking, reading, standing, sitting, writing or talking than you can take? Suppose you spend much time and money studying computer programming only to discover, after you are hired, that your eyes can't take staring into a lighted screen six hours a day. Possessing the right abilities and interests won't do you much good.

♥ BIORHYTHMS: Are you in peak form in the morning, afternoon, early evening or after midnight? If your peak hours are not within the traditional 9-to-5 work schedule, consider working for companies which operate on flextime schedules or which have work at home assignments.

WHAT KIND OF PERSON ARE YOU? If the interviewer doesn't ask this question outright, you can be sure it's always in the back of his/her mind. Employers know from trial and error what psychologists have learned from research:

Career choices are generally good indicators of personality, and vice versa.

People do their best in work which is compatible with their abilities, interests and personality. Two persons may have an equally high aptitude for mechanical work. One is introverted; the other is expressive and enjoys being with people. The first is better suited for a job in an auto repair shop. The second will enjoy teaching mechanics or shop in a vocational or high school.

Psychological studies indicate that people change very little in basic personality traits and occupational interests from their late teens until old age. When they change jobs, they tend to stay within the same job family. A manufacturer's representative is more likely to go into retail sales than into library work.

HOW WOULD YOU DESCRIBE YOUR BASIC COGNITIVE-PERSONALITY TRAITS? This may be the hardest part of your self-assessment, but you have already done much of the work in earlier exercises.

Ask your family members or best friends to make a list of your salient personality characteristics as they see you.

Or, tape record a brief autobiography. Focus on the following events in each of these developmental phases: childhood, adolescence, youth, the present. Watch for traits that recur throughout all phases

* Work
* School
* Friendships
* Play and other leisure activities

Be sure to include traits you might consider not so positive such as: tend to fly off the handle easily, moody, a loner, daydreamer.

Even negative traits can be job related. For example, a person who flies off the handle easily is better off in a job where there is little pressure (e.g., few deadlines, little contact with a demanding public).

Moody? Stay away from jobs which require you to flash a toothpaste smile, to back slap and glad hand your way through day when you feel rotten.

Daydreamer? Jobs which demand attention to detail and a straight-line, logical mind (e.g., bookkeeper, computer programmer, accountant) may not be as fulfilling as jobs requiring imagination and creativity (e.g., advertising copywriter, illustrator, researcher).

Loner? Stay away from jobs that throw you into the thick of social interaction (e.g., sales, entertainment, management).

IT'S IMPORTANT TO HIGHLIGHT TRAITS WHICH MATCH THE REQUIREMENTS OF THE JOB. A computer programmer's cognitive-personality traits would include:

* Analytic, logical mind
* Orderly, organized
* Good at details
* Methodical
* Enjoy working alone
* Enjoy solving problems

You would then illustrate these traits with events from your past:

"Even as a teenager I preferred working at math or crossword puzzles to being a cheerleader."

"My teachers always told me how well organized my written assignments were."

"I've always preferred hobbies which allow me to work things out for myself." (e.g., coin or stamp collecting, inventing things, building model airplanes, building a radio or home computer from a kit.)

"In team sports I always found it more interesting to analyze and plan strategies than to actually get involved in the game."

"My favorite game is chess. "

If, on the other hand, you're applying for a job as copywriter in an advertising agency, you would focus on skills, talents, personality traits and life experiences which match this occupation.

"I was always creative as a child. I ...." (e.g., drew cartoons, wrote poetry, joined a pen pal club, contributed articles for the school newspaper).

"In college I ...." (e.g., made posters and/or wrote short stories) for the college newspaper.

"As a volunteer for the PTA, I wrote the speeches and the copy for ads in the community newsletter."

"My hobbies include crossword puzzles, reading and writing poetry. My favorite game is Scrabble. I still write to my pen pals."

PEOPLE WHO SCORE HIGH IN CERTAIN PERSONALITY TRAITS PREFER CERTAIN OCCUPATIONS OVER OTHERS, psychological studies show.

EXTROVERTS do better as:
* Salesperson   * Marriage counselor
* Advertising executive   * Sales manager
* Manufacturer's representative

OPEN, CURIOUS people do well in inves-
tigative and research occupations such as:
* Journalist
* Librarian   * Social worker
* Free lance writer   * Psychologist
                                 * Scientist

PEOPLE WHO SCORE LOW ON "OPENNESS"
show more interest in:
* Farming   * Funeral Directing
* Banking   * Printing
* Other conventional occupations

ADVERTISING attracts people with these
characteristics: creative, high initiative, high energy,
competitive, works best under pressure, imaginative.

BUSINESS EXECUTIVES, SPORTS PROMO-
TERS, SALESPERSONS AND ENTERTAINERS
tend to exhibit high energy, attention seeking, self-
confidence.

OCCUPATIONS CAN BE GROUPED INTO SIX
BASIC PERSONALITY TYPES, writes psychologist J.L. Holland. Each shows similar patterns of
interests. Many persons show a mixture of two or more.
The following are "pure" types. (The following illustra-
tions are examples from Holland's *Self-Directed Search
Inventory*. See the Appendix for more information.)

ENTERPRISING: ambitious, self-confident,
domineering, energetic, impulsive, commanding.
* Sales   * Buyer
* Manager/executive   * Media producer

CONVENTIONAL: Efficient, conforming, or-
derly, cautious, persistent, self-controlled, unimagina-
tive; prefer to carry out orders rather than to create
and delegate them.

* Clerical	* Tax analyst
* Bank teller	* Banker
* Secretary	* Accountant

REALISTIC: Practical, stable, competitive, conforming; with good physical coordination; prefer working with things rather than with people or ideas; enjoys working with hands, weak verbal and social skills.

* Farmer	* Skilled trades
* Surveyor	* Technical jobs

INVESTIGATIVE: Creative, independent, introverted, curious, analytical, rational; weak leadership skills; enjoys solving problems.

Any occupation which involves research and scientific interests such as chemist, anthropologist, journalist, investigative reporter, market researcher.

ARTISTIC: Imaginative, impulsive, non-conforming, emotional, original, creative, risk taking; prefer to work alone.

* Actor	* Photographer
* Writer	* Composer
* Interior decorator	

SOCIAL: Idealistic, persuasive, undertanding, tactful, cheerful, cooperative, friendly; prefer working in groups to working with things or in solitary problem solving.

* Teacher	* Counselor
* Clergy	* Speech therapist
* Social worker	

@ OBS I WOULD LIKE TO HAVE: On the last sheet identify other occupations which require your abilities, knowledge, training and experience. In times of rapid change, this is better than money in the bank. You need to be ready and willing to plunge into a new job category or to adapt to changes in your present one before it becomes obsolete. The skills and knowledge required in one occupation can often be transferred to others.

A woman who left her job as staff aide with an over-seas United Nations mission found satisfying work as an administrative assistant in a large U.S. corporation. The same skills and experience were applicable: planning, arranging and scheduling conferences, trips and business luncheons.

Music teachers who haven't been able to find jobs in their field have successfully transferred their analytic skills and outgoing personality to computer sales, management and distribution. The more introverted musicians have found success as computer programmers. A former high school music teacher found a job as salesman for a computer corporation and later went into his own distribution business. He loves his new career, especially the oodles of money it brings.

Many older engineers haven't been able to find jobs because new technology has made their training obsolete. Some have successfully transferred their valuable analytic and quantitative abilities, high intelligence and technical skills to other careers

They find jobs as managers in high-tech companies, as mathematics or science teachers, in computer sales and in the financial departments of high-tech companies.

Despite the recent sharp decline in jobs for a Bachelor of Arts degree, there are plenty of opportunities for persons who aren't afraid of change.

Their communication skills and creative thinking and problem solving abilities are valued in advertising, training and development, management, teaching and writing for high-tech and scientific publications. (Scientists and engineers are notoriously poor writers for the lay reader.)

Look at *The Occupational Outlook Handbook* and other guides listed in the Appendix to help you find occupations that are related to the job you are looking for.

IT'S ALSO SMART TO NOTE CHANGES THAT ARE LIKELY TO OCCUR IN YOUR PRESENT OCCUPATION IN THE NEXT THREE TO FIVE YEARS. This should be a cinch if you have done the research recommended in chapter two. For example, future-looking artists, advertising illustrators, architects, interior decorators and draftsmen know they will be working with computers, graphics software and laser printers.

Mid-level managers in insurance or banking know that "intelligent computers" and management software will soon be doing much of the heavy problem solving and that worker participation groups may make their pre-high-tech training obsolete.

LIST THE NEW SKILLS AND KNOWLEDGE YOU NEED IN ORDER TO KEEP UP WITH EXPECTED CHANGES IN YOUR OCCUPATION (or, to transfer to a new one). Make a detailed plan of the steps you need to take in order to accomplish this. For example:

Self-learning through journals, magazines, browsing in the library.

Enrolling in evening adult education class or in a home study course.

IF YOU NEED OUTSIDE HELP:

Aptitude and interest measures help increase your self-awareness so you'll be able to make a better career choice. However, they cannot predict whether you'll succeed in any one occupation. That's because intelligence, motivation, energy level, and other personality related factors are involved.

If the results of these measures support your other qualifications for the job, be sure to tell the interviewer. People in personnel generally have studied and appreciate the significance of psychological tests.

APTITUDE TESTS help estimate what you can do, or learn to do, best. Different occupations require a different combination of aptitudes. Teaching, for example, requires good verbal communication skills, creative thinking, reasoning and other abilities in

addition to knowledge of the subject matter taught.

Aptitude tests can uncover abilities you never realized you had, abilities which are needed in more than one occupation. For the most part, aptitudes are natural, rather than learned, abilities (e.g., music; manual dexterity; spatial, verbal and numerical reasoning).

INTEREST INVENTORIES: The rationale of these measures is that people who share similar interests tend to choose similar occupations. For example, research shows that nurses who are successful and happy in their occupation share a pattern of interests that differ from those of successful real estate salespersons, engineers, computer programmers and accountants.

Some of these inventories can be self-administered. See the Appendix for suggestions.

CAREER COUNSELING SERVICES can help you choose an appropriate occupation. They do it through personal counseling and by administering psychological measures (aptitudes, interests and personality).

They can also show you how to improve your resume and interview skills. Some also provide counseling to help resolve personal and family problems resulting from unemployment. Referrals to on-the-job training may also be involved.

-6-
POLISH
YOUR
IMAGE

YOUR INTERVIEW RATING DEPENDS A LOT ON THE IMAGE YOU PROJECT. Often it's the deciding factor. Because we are a nation of strangers, we Americans rely a lot on surface appearance. Image has such a powerful impact that corporations pay image consultants as much as $225 an hour to create the look of success for their officers.

YOUR TOTAL IMAGE IS COMPRISED OF:

Wardrobe	Energy Level
Grooming	Intelligence
Body Language	State of Health
Speech and Voice Tone	

WARDROBE AND GROOMING ARE IMPORTANT COMPONENTS OF YOUR IMAGE. According to psychological studies, this alone can tip the scales toward hiring or rejecting an applicant.

You would think the basic rules of dress and grooming are practiced by every job hunter who is sound of mind. The New York State Jobs Service describes a teenage applicant who showed up at his first interview dressed in dirty sneakers; worn, faded jeans; shoulder-length hair; and an old sweat shirt. His appearance communicated to the employer a "don't give a damn" attitude.

PROPER ATTIRE AND GROOMING ALSO BOOSTS YOUR SELF-CONFIDENCE.

YOU DON'T HAVE TO SPEND A FORTUNE TO LEARN HOW TO ENHANCE YOUR IMAGE. Common sense and the advice of a trusted friend and/or salesperson can work miracles for you.

THE BASIC RULES OF DRESS AND GROOMING include the following.

DO's:
* Bathed and shaved
* Well fitted suit, neither tight nor baggy
* Shined, "serious" shoes with no run-down heels
* Clean, pressed clothes with no holes or rips
* Hair combed and lightly sprayed, if necessary, to control stray wisps

DON'Ts:
* Heavy makeup
* Leisure wear
* Gum chewing, smoking
* Elaborate, teased hairdo
* Beards or five-o'clock shadow
* Bare legs (even if it's 100 degrees outside)

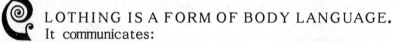 LOTHING IS A FORM OF BODY LANGUAGE. It communicates:
* Social status (kings and millionaires dress differently from peasants and paupers.)
* Occupational status ("blue collar," "hard hat," "banker chic")
* Interests and values (the no-nonsense attire of the prim librarian vs. the same librarian dressed up for the singles bar.)

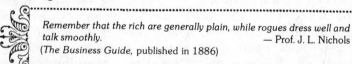

Remember that the rich are generally plain, while rogues dress well and talk smoothly. — Prof. J. L. Nichols
(The Business Guide, published in 1886)

A person's attire may even contradict his/her words and actions. For example, the teenager who dutifully reported to the job interview might as well have stayed home. Deep down inside, he really didn't want the job.

LIKE IT OR NOT, THE CORPORATE UNIFORM EXISTS. Follow the crowd, no matter how much you dislike being swallowed up by the anonymity. The following are some comments made by Yale graduates who were entering the cold, cruel world of job hunting in the Northeast.

"I'm not taking any chances."

"It's playing the game. It's being what they want."

"Everyone wears all cotton or wool in investment banking."

"I stuck out like a sore thumb." (Young woman who wore a sweater and skirt to her first interview.)

"The most boring piece of clothing ever; but by wearing it, I'm announcing my commitment to the world of banking."

DRESS AS IF YOU MEAN BUSINESS, not as if you were headed for the tennis court or beach. If you don't know the dress code of the company or industry you hope to get into, wear a business suit. This goes for women as well as men.

DO NOT wear jeans, sweaters and skirts, culottes, sweat shirts, T-shirts, jogging suit or anything resembling leisure wear.

The fashion gurus now say it's okay for career women to wear tailored dresses. Until this new dictate becomes widespread, however, it's safer to stick to the tailored suit, softened with feminine touches such as pockets placed on the slant to emphasize a narrow waist and blouses with bow ties or ruffled or lace collars.

If it's freezing outside,

91

women may substitute a good quality pantsuit for a skirt and jacket.

HOW STRICTLY SHOULD YOU FOLLOW THE ADVICE FROM FASHION GURUS? It depends on the industry, company, region in which you are looking for a job, and where you stand on the occupational ladder.

THE CLASSIC BUSINESS SUIT GENERALLY PREVAILS AMONG COMPANIES IN THE TRADITIONAL INDUSTRIES (e.g., banking, insurance, oil, utilities, finance).

A TREND TOWARD MORE CASUAL BUSINESS ATTIRE IS SEEN IN:
* High technology firms
* Small (mom and pop) companies
* Certain regions and cities of the nation
* Creative industries (television, advertising, public relations, entertainment)

A trend toward greater casualness, comfort and individuality in business attire is being set by the "baby boomers," 56 million of whom had invaded the workforce in 1984-85. They were the most influenced by the counter revolution of the Sixties, and now they are in the vanguard of the high-tech revolution. The casual attire reflects their attitude that doing work that is interesting and a challenge is more important than possessing the trappings of power.

The new, high-tech companies (e.g., electronics, information processing, bioengineering, cable television) have a higher proportion of young professionals and executives who follow the more relaxed dress code. They've even been seen wearing beards and long hair, bright colors, blue jeans, sweat shirts and sneakers to work.

When one of the high-tech companies recruited an executive of Hooker Chemicals & Plastics Corporation, the culture clash became apparent in the executive's attire. He continued to wear a tie instead of the standard, open neck sport shirt. His colleagues thought he was a snob and his dress habits were even mentioned in the company newsletter.

OLDER PERSONS WHO HOPE TO FIND WORK IN A HIGH-TECH FIRM must decide whether to follow the casual dress code in order to look "cool" or stick to the conservative look. When the Pepsi Cola executive in his forties switched to Apple Computer, he wisely changed to open-neck sports shirts and jeans. His slender figure and boyish looks blended well with the causal attire.

On the one hand, the traditional attire might make older persons look like old timers. On the other hand, a paunchy, 60 year old who wears tight jeans and open neck shirt in order to appear younger creates the opposite impression. It all depends on how trim and youthful you look. Get some advice from a brutally honest friend.

GENERALLY, THE LEADING COMPANY IN AN INDUSTRY SETS THE STANDARD. After the breakup of Bell Telephone, the new AT&T ordered its telephone repairmen and installers to switch from overalls to suit and tie. It wanted to project a new image, similar to that of its chief competitors, IBM and Xerox.

INDIVIDUAL COMPANIES WITHIN AN INDUSTRY MAY FOLLOW THEIR OWN CODE. This is likely to be the case where a company wants to distinguish itself from the leader of the industry in an effort to compete more effectively. Generally, however, the smaller companies try to emulate the leader.

At Merck, a large and well established pharmaceutical company, the suit and tie prevail. But at some of the fast rising biotechnology firms, the "in" attire is blue jeans and tennis shoes.

At IBM, the classic business suit is de rigueur. Its younger rival, Wang, follows a more flexible code, depending on the degree of customer contact an occupation requires.

The movers and shakers of Washington do not wear polyester.
—image consultant

93

DIFFERENT REGIONS OF THE COUNTRY HAVE DIFFERENT VARIATIONS OF THE DRESS CODE (or wherever there are pockets of concentrated, specialized industry). In the Northeast, the "Wall Street Look" sets the pace, particularly in high-finance New York metropolitan region which includes surrounding states.

High-technology centers, such as Silicon Valley in California, Boston's Route 128, and North Carolina's Research Triangle Park, attract young computer nerds, engineers and scientists. This is where the new casual look predominates.

The Southwest leans toward more casual clothes in lighter and brighter colors. The Southeast, like the Northeast, leans toward the conservative look. A pale yellow suit will pass in California but get the boot in New York.

IT ALSO DEPENDS ON THE JOB. Generally, the higher up the occupational ladder, the more conservative the dress code (e.g., blue collar worker-- hard hat, white collar worker--executive look.)

At Wang a business suit is considered more appropriate for persons in jobs which require contact with the public, says Robert J. Awkward, Human Resources Manager. These include sales, marketing, human resources, finance and accounting. But in other positions, such as research and development, casual attire is acceptable.

WHEN IN DOUBT, PLAY IT SAFE. Wear a business suit. Even in some high-tech firms where casual attire is more compatible with their open, informal style, a business suit is considered appropriate for a job interview.

Generally, you're on safe ground if you dress like the boss in the company you want to work in. Most companies want to project a certain image to the public, one which is set by the chief executive officers. They look for employees who are walking advertisements of that image.

Browse through the business magazines and business sections of major city newspapers. Study photographs of

94

company officers for clues on the dress code. Don't be surprised to see Lee Iacocca, CEO of Chrysler Corporation, dressed in the classic business suit and the officers of Apple Computer Company in jeans and sport shirt.

STAND OUTSIDE THE COMPANY AT LUNCH OR CLOSING TIME. EAT IN THE COMPANY CAFETERIA OR GO TO THE LOCAL HANGOUT. Observe how the employees are dressed. See if you can pick out the managers and officers. Study their dress, posture, mannerisms and speech, if possible. Most ambitious underlings play "Follow the leader." In the late 1960's, when Henry Ford grew long sideburns, every manager in the Ford Company, including Lee Iacocca, sported sideburns.

WHATEVER THE DRESS CODE, DON'T GO TO THE INTERVIEW LOOKING LIKE A PEACOCK. Your entire outfit should be understated. It should not overpower you.

Do Not Wear trendy clothes, flashy jewelry, snakeskin accessories, cowboy boots, sandals, fringed Indian suede jackets, plaid trousers, velvet blazers, neon-checked jackets or pants, or shirts in loud patterns and brassy colors. Another tip for men from designer Bill Blass: "I can't imagine anything more ghastly. White socks with a dark suit and dark shoes brand you as the yokel of all times."

THE BUSINESS SUIT SHOULD FIT WELL AND FEEL COMFORTABLE. If you've gained weight since you bought it, have the seams let out by a tailor, or buy one that fits better. The skirt and pants should be loose enough to hide unsightly bulges.

A bargain basement suit which fits poorly and feels uncomfortable is no bargain. It will add to your discomfort and stress during the interview. That's the last thing you need. It will also detract from

95

your air of confidence and authority. Try to visualize yourself dressed as Laurel or Hardy and you'll get the picture.

IF YOU CAN'T AFFORD A TOP QUALITY SUIT, have the local tailor adjust a modestly priced one so that it plays up your best features and camouflages your flaws. With the right accessories, it will look almost as good.

THE SUIT SHOULD BE WELL MADE, ESPECIALLY THE JACKET.
* It should not pull across the shoulders or feel tight under the arms. It should lie flat when you are seated.
* Cuffs and hems should be at a fashionable length.
* Buttons should not strain against the buttonholes when the jacket is closed.
* Stripes, plaids and other subtle designs should match at the seams, especially where the pockets meet the jacket and the jacket lapel joins the back part of the collar.

THE MOST APPROPRIATE COLORS are navy and dark gray, either plain or pin-striped. Dark, rich brown also qualifies as a "serious" color. Black is too somber for an interview, unless you are applying for a job as undertaker or diplomat.
Avoid greens, light to medium browns, plaids and light shades in winter. Summer suits can be of lighter shades.

BASIC GUIDE TO SELECTING COLORS: Dark suits go best with light colored shirts and blouses. A good combination might be a navy suit, soft yellow shirt, yellow and navy tie. Summer suits in light shades look best with a softly contrasting blouse, shirt and tie. However, Mortimer Levitt, author of *Class* (Atheneum, 1984) advises against wearing a darker shirt and tie with a medium shade summer suit.

NATURAL FIBERS, LEATHERS AND METALS LEND AN AIR OF AUTHORITY AND SUCCESS.

This applies to your suit, shoes, shirt and tie, blouse, handbag and accessories.

Preferably, the suit should be of pure cotton, linen or wool (never--God forbid--of pure polyester). It should have a dull or matte finish, not shine like a new penny. If cashmere and the finest woolens, linens and silks are beyond your reach, high quality polyester blends which can pass for the real thing are good. In fact, such blends were in evidence at the top designer fashion shows of 1985.

STATUS CONSCIOUS INTERVIEWERS NO-TICE DETAILS SUCH AS BUTTONS AND BUTTONHOLES. Plastic dime store buttons will brand you as a low person on the totem pole. A bargain basement suit immediately rises in social status when its plastic buttons are replaced with leather, bone or tortoise ones. Hand-stitched buttonholes place you in the jet set class whereas machine made ones relegate you to the masses. Frayed, machine made buttonholes can be spruced up by some deft hand stitching.

A MODERATELY PRICED SUIT LOOKS MORE EXPENSIVE when worn with top quality shoes, belt and handbag, simple but real jewelry (including your watch) and a good quality shirt and tie or blouse.

THE MONOTONY OF THE BASIC BUSINESS SUIT CAN BE LIVENED by accessories and the fabric and pattern of the suit, shirt and tie, or blouse.

*J*EWELRY:
WEAR THE REAL THING (GOLD, SIL-VER, PEARL, STONES) IN SMALL QUANTITIES --if you can afford it.

SMALL, FAKE JEWELRY LOOKS MORE GEN-UINE THAN THE BIG, CHUNKY, FIVE-AND-DIME STUFF.

LEAVE JANGLING JEWELRY AT HOME.

APPROPRIATE JEWELRY FOR MEN includes a gold or silver watch, cuff links and college ring. Tie clips were out of style at the time this book was published.

COAT:
KEEP YOUR DRESSY COAT AND FAKE FUR IN THE CLOSET THIS TIME.

THE MOST APPROPRIATE BUSINESS COAT for autumn/spring is the all-weather trench coat, and for winter a navy, dark gray or brown woolen coat.

BELT:
WEAR A GOOD QUALITY, MATTE LEATHER BELT WITH A BUCKLE THAT ISN'T FLASHY.

KEEP IN THE CLOSET: flashy skins, plastic belts, huge fake metal buckles.

MEN, DO NOT WEAR A WHITE BELT, EVEN IN THE SUMMER. It smacks too much of *Guys and Dolls*.

SHOES:
HAVE WORN HEELS AND TOES RE-PAIRED, AND SHINE THE SHOES BEFORE THE INTERVIEW.

KEEP SHOES WITH SYNTHETIC UPPERS AND FLASHY SKINS IN THE CLOSET.

A MAN CAN'T GO WRONG WEARING DARK BROWN OR BLACK WING-TIP OR CAP-TOE SHOES.

BUT HE WILL IF HE WEARS LIGHT SHOES WITH A DARK SUIT.

MEN, LEAVE YOUR MACHO, WESTERN BOOTS AT

WOMEN, LEAVE YOUR SEXY, OPEN TOED, SPIKE HEELS IN THE CLOSET. Wear sensible, serious shoes with a medium or stylishly low heel. You want the interviewer to be listening to what you say, not studying your legs.

EYEGLASSES:
PSYCHOLOGICAL STUDIES SHOW THAT MEN AND WOMEN WHO WEAR GLASSES ARE VIEWED AS MORE INTELLIGENT, HARD WORKING, DEPENDABLE, HONEST AND SUCCESSFUL.

However, some studies suggest that men who wear glasses are seen as followers rather than leaders. In one of these, consumers were shown pictures of men with different combinations of baldness, facial hair, glasses and hair color. The aim was to find out what the public views as the leadership look. All three of the men in the lowest ranking group wore glasses. Of the top three only one wore glasses. (The latter were also older and had no facial hair.)

STYLE AND FASHION ULTIMATELY RULE HOW THE PUBLIC VIEWS MEN WHO WEAR GLASSES.

FASHIONABLE, DARK, HORN RIMMED GLASSES GIVE AN EXECUTIVE LOOK.

DO NOT WEAR OUTMODED FRAMES IF YOU ARE OVER 40. They add years to your looks. Buy a new pair of stylish frames which enhance your best features and counteract any sallow or grayish skin tones.

SOFT, PINK LENSES TEND TO COUNTERACT A WOMAN'S SALLOW COMPLEXION AND MINIMIZE BAGS UNDER THE EYES.

FAR-OUT FRAMES (AVIATOR, WINGED VICTORY, HUGE SIGNET EMBLEMS) ARE NOT

FOR JOB INTERVIEWING.

DO NOT WEAR SUNGLASSES. The interviewer relies on eye-contact for information. Psychological studies show that wearing sunglasses makes the observer uneasy because they prevent eye contact.

MORE TIPS FOR MEN: THE RIGHT ACCESSORIES EXPRESS YOUR DISTINCTIVE STYLE: a silk foulard pocket square which lends a splash of color; gold or silver, plain or jeweled cuff links; antique pocket watch and chain; shirt and tie.

IF YOU WANT TO PLAY IT SAFE, wear a shirt with either a short-point collar or a button-down collar.

IF YOU WANT TO LOOK MORE YOUTHFUL, wear a rounded or club collar.

THE SHIRT COLLAR LENGTH SHOULD BE IN PROPORTION TO YOUR NECK LENGTH (i.e., the shorter or longer the neck, the shorter or longer the collar).

BRING A FRIEND ALONG WHEN YOU GO SHOPPING for accessories, or ask the salesperson to help you select the most becoming colors and patterns that go with your suit. Wear your business suit so you can get the overall picture.

STICK TO SIMPLE SHIRT PATTERNS. The most business-like patterns are checks (tattersall, pin, box, miniature) and stripes (pin, pencil, hairline, shadow, Bengal and blends). Some fashion experts say you might get away with a boldly striped shirt worn with a classic business suit. It depends on your height and weight. You don't want to go to the interview looking like a barber pole or a pickle barrel.

THE SAFEST SHIRT COLORS are plain white and pale blue, followed by light gray and ivory. You'll be treading on thin waters if you wear pale pink or a colored shirt with white collar and cuffs.

A PIN COLLAR HIDES NECK WRINKLES.

AVOID: Socks that are so short they reveal skin; shirt sleeves that fall below the wrist; trousers that are too short and show socks and shoe tops.

YOU MUST WEAR A TIE WITH A BUSINESS SUIT.

THE TIE MUST HARMONIZE WITH THE SHIRT AND SUIT. A basic rule to follow is to wear a distinctively patterned tie with a plain shirt; a solid color tie with a patterned or pastel shirt. If you want to play it safe, keep the tie simple (e.g., a solid navy tie with a dark gray suit and light blue shirt.)

For a detailed discussion of which tie patterns, colors and tie knots go with different collar shapes, read one of the good books or magazines on men's business wear. See the Appendix.

Never wear a patterned shirt and tie with a suit made of patterned fabric (e.g., herringbone suit, striped shirt, foulard tie). A safe bet is to have only one of these components in a pattern, preferably the shirt or tie. A man with exquisite taste and lots of money can get away with two patterned components.

MORE TIPS FOR WOMEN:
WORKING WOMEN MUST TAKE MORE CARE IN LOOKING BUSINESS-LIKE OR PROFESSIONAL. Though she may be vice-president of a company, her male colleagues may still think of her as "a bit of fluff." This was the finding of a Wall Street Journal/Gallup survey.

IMAGE CONSULTANTS ADVISE WOMEN WHO ARE TRYING TO BREAK INTO MANAGEMENT LEVEL JOBS TO LOOK AS MUCH AS POSSIBLE LIKE THE MALE EXECUTIVE OFFICERS. However, once they get to

101

the top, they tend to relax and wear bright colors, dresses, and even nail polish and dangling earrings at the office. As you learned in Sociology I--The "upper class" generally gets away with breaking middle class notions of propriety.

Don't be surprised to see more women in top positions wearing softer, more feminine and distinctive attire. As more women reach positions of power, there is less need to look like clones of successful men.

CONSIDER HAVING A PROFESSIONAL HAIR STYLE, MAKEUP, AND CLOTHING CONSULTATION. The boost to your self-confidence alone will be worth the cost. One study suggests that with an improved appearance, a female job applicant can get from an 8 to 20% higher salary offer.

PLAY THE GAME BY MEN'S RULES. (Otherwise a male interviewer faced with a great pair of legs, shod in open-toed shoes with spike heels may visualize the wearer in the bedroom rather than the boardroom.)

THE MORE CURVACEOUS YOU ARE, the more attention to dressing so as to emphasize your business-like, no-nonsense qualities. The ultimate horror is to go to the interview looking like Dolly Parton in the movie, *Nine-to-Five*.

AVOID ANYTHING WHICH SUGGESTS SEXINESS:

Sweater	No bra
Perfume	Naked legs
Mini-skirt	Tight skirt
Spike heels	Open-toe shoes
Heavy makeup	See-through blouse
Clinging fabric	Bedroom look hair style
Plunging neckline	Skirt slit to the thigh
Dangling earrings	Talon length fingernails

BEST COLORS FOR A WOMAN'S BUSINESS SUIT are blue, gray, burgundy, beige, black and brown.

CARRY A GOOD QUALITY LEATHER BAG. Leave the shiny vinyl, canvas or satin-look bags at home.

THE SIZE OF THE BAG SHOULD BE IN PROPORTION TO YOUR HEIGHT. A petite woman lugging an overnight-size bag looks as silly as a statuesque woman carrying a tiny clutch.

FOR THE EXECUTIVE LOOK, CARRY A LEATHER PORTFOLIO. If you must take a purse also, put it in the briefcase or portfolio.

NEVER CARRY A TOTE BAG, SHOPPING BAG OR KNAPSACK TO THE INTERVIEW. If you must take one with you, ask the secretary or receptionist to keep it in a safe place until you are ready to leave. Or, put it in your briefcase.

HAIR:
SHOULD YOU DYE THOSE GRAY HAIRS? Until recently, the answer would have been a resounding, "Yes!" Now, however, changing political forces resulting from the graying of America's population are creating new values. Witness the popularity of beautiful, silver haired models like Carmen. Hair stylists are seeing more young men who want silver streaks added to their locks.

It depends on the company and the industry you want to work for. In traditional, conservative companies (such as insurance, financial, oil, utilities and banking) a gray or white haired job applicant will appear more mature and responsible. The same man applying for a job in one of the new, high-tech firms, however, might be viewed as being "over the hill."

The study on consumer views of leadership in men mentioned above revealed that simply changing a man's hair color from black to gray raised his aggregate score for "presidential, believable and interesting" from 33 percent to 67 percent.

According to a Clairol sponsored study, however,

people view gray-haired women as "being older and having less energy."

It ultimately depends on how the rest of the woman looks. Gray or silver tinted hair, done in an up-to-date style, looks striking on a slender body and youthful face. It's one way to stand out from the crowd.

A silver-haired woman of sixty, still elegant and glamorous, applied for a job with a Wall Street firm where most of the employees were under 35. She was hired as a facilities planner at a starting salary of $38,000. "We need someone with your maturity," the personnel manager told her.

IF YOU DECIDE TO COVER THE GRAY, A SOFTER SHADE THAN YOUR ORIGINAL HAIR COLOR IS MORE FLATTERING AND YOUTHFUL LOOKING. This is because the skin and eyes lose pigmentation as we grow older. Hair coloring that conforms to the older woman's natural hair is more flattering than blue-black or brassy red or blonde hair.

SALT-AND-PEPPER HAIR LOOKS GREAT WHEN WORN WITH A GRAY SUIT WITH SILVER ACCESSORIES AND TOUCHES OF BRILLIANT COLOR (tie, pocket square, blouse).

WHITE HAIR LOOKS STUNNING WITH A BLOUSE AND/OR ACCESSORIES IN CHERRY RED, EMERALD GREEN, BRIGHT BLUE OR PURPLE.

A WOMAN LOOKS OUTDATED AND OLDER if she wears the lacquered, bouffant hair styles of the Fifties, or hair that is flat on top, or too straight, or either too short or too long. The experts recommend ear length or chin length hair, styled to softness.

IF YOU WEAR A WIG, MAKE SURE IT'S OF GOOD QUALITY. Dime store wigs are aging and almost anyone can tell when you are wearing one.

FINGERNAILS should be filed to business

length. Avoid dirty fingernails, bright nail polish, talon-length or uneven nails.

TIPS FOR PERSONS OVER FORTY

OLDER JOB APPLICANTS MUST MAKE A SPECIAL EFFORT TO LOOK UP-TO-DATE.

AVOID DRAB COLORS IN THE ACCESSORIES. They make an older person look washed out.

ANYTHING THAT IS WORN BY THE HIP CROWD SHOULD STAY IN THE CLOSET. This includes jeans (see above for exceptions to the rule), mini-skirts, open neck shirts that reveal a hairy chest, men's neck chains and charms.

You'll look more youthful in clothing that is in fashion with the mature age crowd. Study the fashions in *Gentleman's Quarterly*, *M*, *Vogue*, *Harper's Bazaar* and other magazines which cater to the affluent, mature reader.

TIGHT FITTING CLOTHES MAKE A PERSON APPEAR OLDER.

INSTEAD OF WHITE, WEAR A CREAM OR LIGHT COLORED SHIRT OR BLOUSE. It makes you look more alive. Stark white tends to drain color from the face. Wear it only if you want to look like Count Dracula.

WOMEN, ARE YOU CONCERNED ABOUT NECK WRINKLES? Wear a blouse with a high collar or a becoming scarf.

 What does my hair have to do with my husband's ability to be president?
—Jacqueline Kennedy

EMBARRASSED BY FLABBY UPPER ARMS? Just in case it's hot and the interviewer invites you to take off your jacket, be sure to wear a three quarter length or long sleeve blouse.

SOFT SHADES OF MAKEUP, APPLIED LIGHTLY, are more flattering than either no makeup at all or makeup applied with a heavy hand.

WEAR A LIGHT TEXTURED FOUNDATION, EVEN THOUGH YOU GENERALLY GO WITHOUT IT. It lends a youthful dewiness and minimizes minor flaws such as age spots and uneven skin tones. Avoid heavy pancake foundation. It magnifies skin crevices.

ROSE, PINK OR PEACH SHADES BRIGHTEN YOUR COMPLEXION. Avoid yellowish and brown tones which tend to increase sallowness and make you look wilted.

AVOID FOUNDATION AND POWDER IN SHADES LIGHTER THAN YOUR SKIN. They lend an aura of fatigue and anemia at a time you need to look healthy and brimming with energy.

LUMINESCENT POWDER AND CREAM OR LIQUID ROUGE LEND A YOUTHFUL DEWINESS. Powders and matte finishes heighten the dryness of the skin which increases with age.

HOWEVER, USE MATTE EYESHADOW instead of shiny creams and iridescent powders. The later call attention to crepey eyelids.

THE BASIC RULES TO FOLLOW IN DRESSING FOR THE INTERVIEW ARE:
    * Avoid overdoing it.
    * Avoid underdoing it.
    * Follow the leaders.
    * Focus on the whole, not the parts. (The different parts of your outfit should harmonize: suit, shoes, shirt or blouse, bag/briefcase, ...)

HEALTH AND ENERGY

YOUR APPARENT VITALITY AND STATE OF HEALTH ARE EVEN MORE IMPORTANT TO YOUR OVERALL IMAGE. Even though you wear a Brooks Brothers business suit, if you look fatigued, the employer will wonder whether you have the stamina to do the work.

The nation is currently on a health craze. Many companies sponsor diet and exercise programs for their workers or pay for the cost of enrolling in a health club. There is more than altruism behind this.

Employers find that good health practices increase their workers' productivity, reduce health costs and improve morale. A Johnson & Johnson study found that employees who participated in its health program were absent less often, more satisfied with their jobs, and handled job related stress better.

GO ON A DIET AND EXERCISE PROGRAM IF YOU'RE NOT IN TOP CONDITION. Studies show that people in most Western societies view obese people as less hard working, successful, intelligent, attractive and popular than people who are slender.

EMPLOYERS HAVE INDIRECT WAYS OF ESTIMATING YOUR HEALTH AND STAMINA. One is the job application form which asks for your height and weight. (That's why it's best to leave this out of your resume if your weight is out of proportion to your height.) Another way is to observe the way you walk into the room and sit down. The pace in which you answer questions also is a clue to your energy level.

GET A MEDICAL CHECKUP IF YOU FEEL TIRED AND DEPRESSED MUCH OF THE TIME.

IF THE DOCTOR FINDS NOTHING WRONG WITH YOU PHYSICALLY, THE PROBLEM

MAY BE PSYCHOLOGICAL. A cause of persistent fatigue may be boredom with one's occupation. Anxiety and lack of confidence about changing careers and/or a job may also be the culprit.

YOUR FACE, POSTURE AND GESTURES REFLECT ANY FATIGUE, DEPRESSION AND ANXIETY. If this is your problem, see the chapter seven (nonverbal communication) to learn how to camouflage the signs. Read chapter ten for tips on how to attain a positive, self-confident attitude. Read chapter five to learn if you are in the right career. If your interests, abilities and personality do not match the demands of your occupation and/or the company you work for, this also contributes to a general lassitude and depression.

7

HOW TO BE MORE CONVINCING: THE TRICKS OF BODY LANGUAGE

"THE BODY DOESN'T LIE," writes J. Fast. The words we speak may say one thing while our body "says" something contradictory. An applicant may lie about the reason for a job dismissal. As he speaks, however, the interviewer may notice he avoids eye contact or looks fixedly at him. The applicant's body may become tense, and his face flushed.

More than 55% of our inner thoughts and feelings are revealed through body language. In a face-to-face conversation, words carry approximately 7% of meaning; the rest is carried through voice tone and body language.

This "Silent Language," as Edward Hall calls it, involves the way we sit, stand, cross our legs, fold our arms, and make gestures and facial expressions. It also involves eye contact and the way we "use" space.

The power of nonverbal communication was shown in a study in which experienced educators were fooled into believing they had learned worthwhile information from a lecture given by a phony "Dr. Fox." Actually, "Dr. Fox's" words made no sense. He had been instructed beforehand to give irrelevant, meaningless and contradictory information while, at the same time, using a prestige-laden body language.

THE POWER OF NONVERBAL COMMUNICA-
TION LIES IN THE FACT THAT WE USU-
ALLY ARE NOT CONSCIOUS OF WHAT OUR
BODY IS "SAYING." Much of an actor's
training is learning how to control (i.e., make him/her-
self conscious of) his body language. Ronald Reagan is a
master at this. Notice how he crinkles up his eyes and
smiles broadly at a gathering, how he ever so slightly
leans forward in a warm, accepting manner, with arms
outstretched, palms up, and head cocked in the manner of
a lover gazing at a beloved.

*If you could meet Winnie, you'd think she is bizarre.
She can think and do a job. She has a bachelor's degree
in sociology...but she doesn't smile. She holds the
upper part of her body very rigid. Who wants to work
with her? We have videotaped her. We have told her
simple things like, when she looks at someone to look
away every now and then, to smile and move her body. --*
Janet Roberts, executive director of the Women's Survival Center in Tampa, Florida.

JOB INTERVIEWERS, LIKE COUNSELORS
AND DETECTIVES, ARE TRAINED TO
DETECT AND INTERPRET NONVERBAL COMMU-
NICATION. Stella Norman describes some of
the things a counselor notices about a client before any
words are spoken: [6]
   ♥ In The Waiting Room: Is the client pacing the
floor? If the client is sitting, does he/she appear
comfortable, tense or defensive? What is the client
doing--reading, fidgeting, smoking nervously?
   ♥ Introduction: Does a handshake (or lack of one)
seem to disturb the client? Does the client exhibit
trust or distrust?
   ♥ The Client's Walk: Observe the way the client
walks into the office. A depressed person walks with
head down and feet shuffling along. A preoccupied one
walks slowly, hands behind back, one hand clasped over
the other. A confident person walks with head up; a
firm, jaunty step; shoulders back and arms swinging.

110

♥ In The Office: Where does he/she sit when offered a choice of chairs? Near the interviewer or as far away as possible? What is his/her sitting posture? Does the client make eye contact? Does he sit facing toward or away from the counselor?

A PREOCCUPATION WITH YOUR BODY LANGUAGE DURING THE INTERVIEW MAY CREATE A MENTAL BLOCK. The way to avoid self-consciousness is to practice more effective ways of communicating until they seem natural. Rehearse the interview in front of a mirror; better yet, videotape it. Visualize yourself as a poised and effective communicator, going through all the right motions in your mind. Eventually, you will become one. However, if you wait until the day or evening before an important interview, it may do more harm than good.

FACIAL EXPRESSIONS ARE EASIER TO CONTROL THAN BODY MOVEMENTS AND GESTURES, studies show. Most of us can put on a smiling, self-confident and innocent face, but it takes a lot of practice to learn how to voluntarily control our hands (clenched fists), fingers (twitching, drumming), feet (twisted tightly together) and posture (stooped, tense). Such signs are a dead giveaway of a person's true feelings.

ℱACIAL EXPRESSIONS

FACIAL EXPRESSIONS GIVE THE INTERVIEWER VALUABLE CLUES TO YOUR DEEPEST FEELINGS AND REACTIONS. When discussing sensitive issues, such as how you got along with your former boss and why you quit or were dismissed from a job, the interviewer is especially alert to the signs on your face. Tightened jaw muscles usually indicates antagonism; eye squinting suggests dislike, hostility; a frown may result from displeasure or confusion.

111

SHOULD YOU PLAY IT SAFE AND PUT ON A POKER FACE? The answer is "No!" Studies show that people who are expressive are viewed as more honest and trust- worthy, more sociable and emotionally open. People who want to suppress nonverbal signals which reveal infor- mation about their thoughts often put on a poker face. Now you know why actors who portray executives and detectives are generally poker faced.

JOB APPLICANTS WHO ARE RESPON- SIVE AND EXPRESSIVE, WHO GESTURE FREELY, MAKE A BETTER IMPRESSION. They are also rated as being more effective at persuading others. This is very important in some occupations.

HOWEVER, PEOPLE WHO APPEAR TOO EAGER, WHO ARE OVER-RESPONSIVE, MAY BE VIEWED AS IMPULSIVE, NEUROTIC OR DOMINEERING. Like all else in life, too much of a good thing can be bad for you.

EXPRESSIVENESS IS VERY IMPORTANT IN OCCUPATIONS WHICH REQUIRE MOTIVA- TING, INSPIRING, INFLUENCING AND LEAD- ING OTHERS (e.g., sales, teaching, acting, counseling, politics and the clergy). One study found that the top Toyota salesman in the country in 1980 scored 99% on a test of responsiveness. If you are applying for a job as chef, forklift operator or oceano- grapher, you can skip this section. But if the job you want requires teamwork and influencing people, read on.

SMILE AND ESTABLISH EYE CONTACT AS YOU SHAKE HANDS. Do this when you greet the interviewer and when you are about to leave. Also, smile at appropriate times during the interview. Smiling expresses warmth and interest.

SMILE, BUT DON'T OVERDO IT, LADIES.
Research shows that women are more expressive and smile
significantly more often than men. This is appropriate
when tending a baby or gazing at a lover, but it's
woefully out of place in a job interview. It can be seen
as a sign of submissiveness and dependency.

Women managers who smile a lot are viewed by their
male colleagues as less effective and less likely to
succeed, one study found. Older women, especially, need
to learn that the business and professional world can be
a jungle. It's not like the home and community where
emotional bonding plays an important role in social
interactions.

**WHEN A PERSON IS TRYING TO DECEIVE,
THE FACE MAY DISPLAY SEVERAL CON-
TRADICTORY EMOTIONS AT THE SAME TIME.**
Counselors are trained to be on the lookout for the
following:

Does the entire face express the same message? (ge-
nuine interest in the job)

Does one area of the face display one emotion while
another area displays a different one? (smiling mouth
and narrowed, distrustful eyes)

Do the facial expressions match other nonverbal and
verbal messages? (Not if the face eager while the tone
of voice is flat.)

**ᗷ ACK OF EYE CONTACT MAKES THE INTER-
VIEWER UNEASY** because it deprives him/her
of an important source of information. For example, the
eyes express confidence, guilt, fear and forgiveness.

DO NOT WEAR SUNGLASSES TO THE INTERVIEW.

**LOOK AT THE INTERVIEWER WHEN YOU
ANSWER QUESTIONS.** Don't look at the wall,
floor or at your watch. Too little eye contact may be
interpreted as rudeness, shyness, as not wanting to
communicate or, worse yet, as trying to deceive.

**EYE CONTACT MAKES THE OBSERVER MORE
COMPLIANT,** psychological studies show. A

researcher who posed as a panhandler found that passersby were more likely to give a handout when he established eye contact with them than when he averted his eyes.

INTERVIEWERS RATE PEOPLE WHO MAKE EYE CONTACT MORE HIGHLY THAN THOSE WHO DON'T. Eye contact in face-to-face encounters is a sign of mutual respect.

LOOK AWAY FROM TIME TO TIME WHILE TALKING OR LISTENING TO THE INTERVIEWER. Avoid a steady, unwavering gaze. It communicates hostility, aggression and insult. "In our society, eye contact with a stranger for longer than 3 seconds is considered to be rude; for longer than 10 seconds it's insulting or threatening," writes Stella Norman.

WANT TO APPEAR CONFIDENT? WALK INTO THE ROOM WITH YOUR HEAD HELD HIGH, SHOULDERS BACK AND SPINE STRAIGHT. Picture an actor attempting to convey a sense of worthlessness and defeatism without uttering a word--shoulders hunched, head bowed, lips down at the corners and brows knitted. An alert interviewer picks up such signals.

SHAKE HANDS FIRMLY, BUT GENTLY, WITH A FULL PALM. Never shake hands with your fingertips. It makes you appear prissy and overly fastidious, as if you were afraid of catching the interviewer's germs.

SIT WITH YOUR HEAD HELD HIGH. If you allow it to sink into your shoulders, you'll look like a frightened ostrich.

HOLD YOUR HANDS CUPPED IN YOUR LAP, PALMS UP, AND YOU'LL CONVEY AN INTERESTED, INVITING, FRIENDLY ATTITUDE. Or, rest them lightly on the arms of the chair. Open palms convey acceptance, a willingness to listen.

AVOID THE FOLLOWING so as not to create an aura of tension, fear, anxiety and hostility.

* Crack your knuckles.
* Fiddle with your hair.
* Smoke a cigar or cigarette.
* Swing a leg or jiggle a foot.
* Clench your hands into a fist.
* Stand with your hands on your hips.
* Clear your throat often and loudly.
* Grip the arms of the chair tightly.
* Scratch your head from time to time.
* Twirl your thumbs; tap your fingertips.
* Sit with fingers laced tightly together.
* Sit with your arms folded across your chest.
* Clasp your hands across your abdomen or chest.
* Tap or drum on a surface with your fingernails.
* Touch or rub your nose from time to time (People do this subconsciously when they find something disagreeable or disgusting.)
* Put your hand to your mouth as you speak or listen to the interviewer. (Law enforcement officers say this communicates a range of negative emotions from lack of confidence to lying.)
* Tug at your collar every now and then so that you look like a cornered rabbit or as if you've been caught doing something naughty.
* Rub the back of your neck occasionally (a "you're a pain in the neck" message).

NEVER TAKE NOTES DURING THE INTERVIEW UNLESS IT'S TO JOT DOWN FACTS THAT ARE EASILY FORGOTTEN. It can be misinterpreted as arrogance, lack of assurance, or poor memory.

WOMEN, SIT WITH YOUR LEGS CROSSED AT THE ANKLES. Placing your legs apart, even slightly, sends a subtle, sexual signal which is inappropriate to a job interview.

$\mathcal{S}$PACE ALSO SPEAKS

PEOPLE USE SPACE TO COMMUNICATE AU-
THORITY AND SOCIAL STATUS, HOSTILITY
AND AGGRESSION, OR INTIMACY AND LOVE.
Space communicates by:

* The distance you place your chair from the interviewer.
* The direction of your seated body vis-a-vis the
  interviewer.
* Physical "barriers placed between you and the
  interviewer.

SIT AT A RESPECTFUL DISTANCE FROM
THE INTERVIEWER, NOT TOO CLOSE OR TOO
FAR AWAY. Sitting too close may be
interpreted as a sign of disrespect, as threatening or
as an unwarranted display of intimacy.

Moving the chair farther away from the spot where the
interviewer asks you to sit may be interpreted as fear,
nervousness, lack of confidence, or as an insulting
dislike or disgust.

SIT IN A RELAXED MANNER AND LEAN, EVER
SO SLIGHTLY, TOWARD THE INTERVIEWER.
This conveys approval, acceptance and self-confidence.
Sitting with your body turned away from the interviewer
communicates fear, distance, dislike.

PUT YOUR PURSE OR BRIEFCASE ON THE
FLOOR, BESIDE YOU. Placing it on your
lap makes you appear to be hiding behind a barricade.

NEVER PLACE YOUR FEET ON THE DESK
OR CHAIR. NEVER LEAN BACK WITH YOUR
HANDS CLASPED BEHIND YOUR NECK. This
communicates an attitude of disrespect and
disinterest as clearly as if you were to
shout it.

A SILENT CODE OF SOCIAL STATUS AND
AUTHORITY IS COMMUNICATED BY WHO IS
ALLOWED TO TOUCH WHOM. If the inter-
viewer places a hand on your shoulder as you leave,

that's okay, since he/she has the higher authority in this situation.

Never, under any circumstance, place your hand or arm on the interviewer. Don't touch the interviewer except for a handshake. If you do, he/she may resent it as a sign of condescension. This is especially serious if the interviewer is much younger than you are.

8

HOW TO BE CONVINCING:
LEARN TO SPEAK
MORE EFFECTIVELY

THE WAY YOU SPEAK STRONGLY INFLUEN-
CES THE INTERVIEWER'S RATING OF YOUR
ABILITIES, PERSONALITY AND INTELLIGENCE.

YOU CAN EASILY IMPROVE YOUR SPEECH
AND VOICE BY TAPE RECORDING A JOB
INTERVIEW REHEARSAL. The first time you
listen to yourself, you'll probably be shocked. Most
people are. Is your voice too high pitched? Is it too
loud? Does it sound harsh or nasal? Don't despair. It
can easily be improved.

VOICE TONE IS AN IMPORTANT COMPONENT
OF SPEECH. Contrast the finishing school
tones of TV anchorwoman Barbara Walters--soft and low
pitched--with the high pitched, loud, nasal tone of
Dingbat of *All In The Family*.

YOU'LL SOUND MORE SELF-ASSURED AND
BUSINESS-LIKE BY LOWERING YOUR VOICE.
Listen to yourself on tape or as you talk with your head
lowered between your knees. Experts say most people

pitch their voices too high, especially when they are under stress-and what is more stressful than a job interview?

Women, especially, are advised to lower their voice and slow down their rate of speaking. They have a tendency to speak too rapidly and in too high a pitch when they're nervous.

A FLAT VOICE TONE MAY TURN OFF THE INTERVIEWER. Psychological studies show that he/she is more likely to be compliant if you speak with an expressive, warm tone.

A LARGE VOCABULARY IS ASSOCIATED WITH CAREER SUCCESS. What does it mean, to have a "large" vocabulary? It means to possess the basic word "tools" with which to express your thoughts clearly, concisely and accurately. It doesn't mean bowling over the interviewer with 4-or-5 syllable words. Not only will you fail to impress him, you'll come across as a pompous egghead.

OMIT JARGON AND JAWBREAKER VOCABU-LARY UNLESS IT'S USED IN THE INDUSTRY. Professionals who are changing careers should especially avoid being seen as ivory tower types who don't belong in the business world.

LEAVE THE SLANG AND BAR ROOM LAN-GUAGE FOR MORE APPROPRIATE SETTINGS. Vice presidential candidate George Bush created a stir when he said "kick some ass" during the 1984 campaign. He barely managed to get away with this, but you won't. Put on your best business manner and speech when you go for an interview.

AVOID POOR GRAMMAR, if you can help it. Ask the friend who helps you rehearse the interview to be on the lookout for such boo-boos as "AIN'T" and double negatives ("I DON'T have NO dependents.")

DON'T ANSWER QUESTIONS WHICH RE-QUIRE A COMPLETE ANSWER WITH A

BLUNT "YES" OR "NO" OR WITH PHRASES. For example, in response to the question, "What did you do from 1979 to 1982?" a poor answer would be, "Odd jobs." A better answer would be to describe in detail your schooling and/or the jobs you've held, your responsibilities and achievements, and your reasons for leaving. Say this in complete, grammatical sentences.

Or, if you are asked, "Does computerized equipment scare you?" don't just say "No." Give examples of your interest in and/or knowledge of this important new technology.

BE CONCISE. THE MORE LONG-WINDED YOU ARE, THE MORE LIKELY TO PUT YOUR FOOT IN YOUR MOUTH. Don't lead up to the punch line in the drawn-out manner of Dingbat. Give the important facts first, followed with some examples if more clarification is needed. Then stop and ask if the interviewer would like more information.

AVOID USING OUTDATED EXPRESSIONS, such as "Gee willikers," "Golly," "Dame," "Broad," or "I'll be darned." Ask a younger member of your family to spot any such speech mannerisms or vocabulary.

LEARN THE BUZZWORDS OF THE INDUSTRY AND OCCUPATION TO SHOW THAT YOU'RE UP TO DATE. Use them at appropriate times during the interview.

SPEAK SO YOU CAN BE HEARD, BUT NOT SO LOUD THAT YOU GIVE THE IMPRESSION OF BEING HARD OF HEARING.

THE MOST BEAUTIFUL SOUND IN THE WORLD IS THE SOUND OF A PERSON'S NAME. Mention

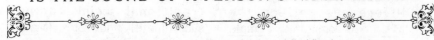

His economy of speech is welcome in a place so full of flatulence.
—a member of the United Nations

121

the interviewer's name when you greet him/her, when you depart, and at appropriate times during the interview.

A SIMPLE NOD OF YOUR HEAD AND AN "UH-HUH" NOW AND THEN AS THE IN- TERVIEWER SPEAKS COMMUNICATES AGREEMENT, WARMTH AND A WILLINGNESS TO LISTEN. If you want the interviewer to get hot under the collar, look steadily into his/her eyes with an expressionless face, and remain completely silent.

IN FACE-TO-FACE ENCOUNTERS, SILENCE COMMUNICATES DISAPPROVAL AND HOSTILITY. It can be more threatening than belligerent words, re- ports Jon Eisenson, Director emeritus of speech patholo- gy at Stanford University School of Medicine.

ANOTHER WAY TO ANTAGONIZE IS TO INTER- RUPT AS THE INTERVIEWER SPEAKS. It's not only rude; it violates an unspoken rule of social status and authority. Sociological studies find that persons of higher status (in this case the interviewer and employer) are allowed to interrupt persons of lower status (job applicants and employees). Interviewers like to think they are in command of the situation. Woe to any applicant who tries to take over.

DO YOU HAVE A HABIT OF ENDING STATE- MENTS WITH A QUESTION MARK AT THE END? It makes you sound dependent and indecisive. The voice should rise only at the end of a question.

WOMEN, AVOID KITCHEN TALK

MEN AND WOMEN SPEAK DIFFERENTLY. They differ in voice tone, in the structure and content of sentences, and in topics of conversation. The differences are so great, say sociologists, that they actually speak a different language even though they use the same vocabulary and grammar, say sociologists. The differences reflect their traditional social status (MALE = dominant; Female = subordinate) and roles (Male = provider, achiever; Female = dependent, nurturer).

Male-female social roles and status are changing so rapidly these days that no one can say for sure what the new rules are. Older women, who grew up to believe that a woman's function is to serve men, will benefit the most from the following tips. In fact, the differences in communication between women over 40 and younger women are probably greater than the male-female differences of today.

WHEN A WOMAN USES A FEMALE MODE OF COMMUNICATING, PEOPLE SUBCONSCIOUSLY DE-VALUE WHAT SHE SAYS. It doesn't matter how impressive are her title and credentials. This was seen in a study of sex differences in communicating while in a courtroom situation. Both male and female jurors, without being aware of it, listened more closely when a man gave testimony than when a woman did. In fact, the woman's comments were more often ignored.

SMART WOMEN PLAY BY MEN'S RULES. Some findings of a Wall Street Journal/Gallup survey of top women executives explain why.[38, 39]

Fifty-three percent of the top women executives who were interviewed said they had to change their personalities in order to succeed. "You have to work really hard not to be the least bit emotional, so they can't say you are behaving 'just like a woman'" said one executive. They learned to be more reserved, serious and business-like. (The male colleagues who resented them most were those who were competing with them for the highest ranking jobs.)

WOMEN'S TALK CONVEYS UNCERTAINTY, TENTATIVENESS AND A SUBORDINATE OR CHILD-LIKE STATUS. Men's talk, on the other hand, communicates competence and authority. It is more direct and assertive and it conveys more factual information. Here are examples of subordinate ways of speaking (by men as well as women).

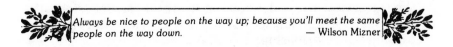

Always be nice to people on the way up; because you'll meet the same people on the way down.
— Wilson Mizner

"I wonder if ...."
"I could be mistaken, but ...."
"I'm not entirely sure, but ...."
"I don't really know the salary range."
"You're probably right." (vs. "You're right.")
"I'm pretty sure I can do the job." (vs. "I'm sure I can do the job.")
"I don't know how accurate this is, but I hear the typical benefits for this job are

IN MIXED SEX GROUPS, MEN TEND TO TALK MORE THAN WOMEN. This inhibits a non-assertive woman and makes it difficult for her to hold her own. One study found the average time used by women at business conferences was less than half that used by men. "Don't sit back and be the smiley one. Let them know you're there or they'll never see you," said a woman executive in the survey.

WOMEN ARE MORE FREQUENTLY INTERRUPTED THAN MEN, AND IT'S THE MEN WHO DO ALMOST ALL THE INTERRUPTING. The women rarely asserted their right to finish and be heard. "It's as if they accept their subordinate status as a natural state of being," concluded the researcher.

TOPICS WHICH ARE INITIATED BY WOMEN ARE RARELY FOLLOWED THROUGH BY MEN, in mixed sex conversations. This often happens even if the woman is a director or professional to whom the men must report.

A WOMAN SHOULD HOLD HER GROUND IF A MALE INTERVIEWER INTERRUPTS OR FAILS TO PICK UP IMPORTANT INFOR- MATION ABOUT HER WORK QUALIFICATIONS.
Use tact, however. Wait for the interviewer to pause before saying, "As I was saying ...." NEVER get angry or berate the interviewer for being rude. NEVER interrupt the interviewer. This can be a fatal error, since it reverses the normal social balance of the interview/interviewee relationship.

124

WOMEN'S TALK IS LESS DIRECT.
A man is more likely to say, "It stinks," whereas a woman prefers to say, "It has a bad smell." A man may say, "... six books," whereas a woman will use approximations such as, "... about six books." The latter gives the impression of uncertainty, lack of confidence, and incompetence.

WOMEN OFTEN CHANGE A DECLARATIVE SENTENCE TO A QUESTION. "It's cold in here, isn't it?" A man, on the other hand, will say "It's cold in here."

WOMEN USE FAR TOO MANY QUALIFIERS: "Perhaps," "I suppose," "probably," "As I interpret it," "I just feel that ...."

WOMEN TEND TO STATE A REQUEST IN THE FORM OF A QUESTION. "May I have a glass of water?" Men, instead, tend to make the request sound like a command: "Give me a glass of water."

WOMEN ARE MORE APT TO COMPOUND A REQUEST. "Won't you please close the door?" Men are more likely to say with authority, "Close the door" or "Close the door, please."

WOMEN MORE OFTEN SAY "PLEASE" AND "THANK YOU." A 1975 survey found that a woman who fails to say this is frowned upon whereas a man is not. (Whether this attitude still exists needs to be tested).

In the meantime, say "Thank you" when you are offered something and also at the end of the interview, but don't overdo it. "Yes, please" sounds submissive; "Yes" sounds more assertive.

NEVER ASK FOR PERMISSION TO SPEAK. For example, "May I ask a question?" casts you in the role of a third grader or a slave. When it's appropriate to interject, go ahead and speak.

WOMEN AGREE, COMPLY, ACCEPT, AND SUPPORT OTHER SPEAKERS ALMOST TWICE AS MUCH AS MEN. Men have acquired the more adaptive jungle tactics of debating, commanding, asserting and lecturing.

"A MAN WHO IS AGGRESSIVE IS CONSIDERED ASSERTIVE. WHEN A WOMAN IS, SHE'S A BITCH," said a female vice president who was interviewed in the Wall Street Journal/Gallup survey. She cautions women not to come on too strong or they may appear threatening to male colleagues.

SUCCESSFUL BUSINESS WOMEN LEARN TO ADAPT, NOT IMITATE, MALE COMPETITIVE TACTICS AND MANNERISMS. The nation's values and beliefs regarding proper behavior are still changing. There are men, chiefly the older managers and executives, who do not take kindly to aggressive women.

Again, it depends on how conservative the company is. Robert Reinhold advises women in high technology companies, "... aggressive isn't a bad word...(Women) need to ask a lot of questions and also to question higher authority." This is fine in a milieu where most of the top brass are under forty. [45]

MEN USE MORE OF THE LATEST BUZZWORDS IN BUSINESS, ECONOMICS AND HIGH-TECH. This makes them appear up-to-date.

HUMOR, IN MODERATION, IS A PLUS FACTOR IN JOB INTERVIEWS, as in political campaigns. Men are also more likely to use humor and witticisms. Whom would you hire, the applicant who displays a keen sense of humor or the one who, although equally qualified, is dour and humorless?

LAUGHING IS ANOTHER MATTER, HOWEVER.
In mixed-sex conversations, women often laugh hardest and longest. Sociologists say this reflects the traditional sex roles of male authority and female compliance and subordination.

MEN USE MORE PROFANITY AND OBSCENITIES
(e.g., "Hell," "damn," and other four-letter words). Women, however, are still expected to set standards of dignity and decorum. Both are advised against using the more redolent expletives.

WOMEN WHO USE SUCH TERMS, IN THE MISTAKEN BELIEF THAT THEY ARE PLAY-ING BY MEN'S RULES, APPEAR OBNOXIOUS TO MEN. It's still a man's world, ladies.
Use softer expletives, if you must, such as "Oh, nuts."

LITTLE OLD LADIES HAVING TEA AND CRUMPETS are associated with antiquated
expressions like "Oh dear," "Gracious," "Dear me," "Heavens to Betsy," and "Oh Fudge."

THERE IS A STEREOTYPE THAT WOMEN DIGRESS MORE IN THEIR CONVERSATIONS.
There is psychological evidence that older women especially tend to speak as if they were painting word pictures. This can be fatal during an interview, where the ability to get to the point quickly is being assessed. It has something to do with left-right brain dominance. Psychological studies show that in addition to age and sex roles, other factors are involved such as social class, education and child rearing.

We want people to understand our "religion." Then we ask them if they are prepared to change religion. If so, we keep them.
—Jack Tramiel, President of Atari Co.

MEN'S TALK IS MORE FACTUAL AND OBJECTIVE.

They use far fewer adjectives and expressive terms which reveal their true feelings. This is in keeping with their greater reluctance to display facial expressions. It's safer in competitive situations like job interviews. It's also more practical in situations where sticky emotions must not interfere with getting the work done.

Women use significantly more words which refer to feelings, emotions and motivation. They use "I" and other expressions of self-reference more often.

See if you can pick out, from the following list, those words men are more likely to use.

awful	pretty	terribly
quite	darling	divine
sweet	adorable	wonderful
heavenly	dreamy	charming
nearly fainted	lovely	beautifully
died laughing	dearest	precious
oh dear	divine	cute
great	terrific	precious
dearest	gracious me	heavens
neat	I could just scream	
oh!	perfectly wonderful	

S YOU REVIEW THIS BOOK, UNDER-
LINE OR MAKE NOTES OF THOSE
TIPS WHICH ESPECIALLY APPLY TO YOU.

1. Old habits and ways of thinking you need to
<u>unlearn</u>.

2. New habits and ways of thinking to <u>learn</u> and
<u>practice</u>.

You might, for example, have to work on certain
questions you may be asked, on your self confidence, on
your speech or voice tone, on nervous mannerisms, and/or
aspects of your appearance.

If you think, "I can find a job without all this
effort," consider this. Any improvement in the way you
present yourself to others will enhance your success and
happiness in other major areas of your life:

* Your self-esteem
* Relations with the opposite sex
* Career advancement AFTER you find a job
* Relations with family members and friends

CHECK THE INTERVIEWER QUESTIONS in
chapter 15 you'll probably be asked and most likely trip

up on.

THEN THINK OF THE ESSENTIAL POINTS TO INCLUDE IN YOUR ANSWER TO EACH QUESTION:

Leave in only what's relevant to the job, the employer's needs and your personal compatibility with the job and the organization.

Leave out non-essential points which waste the interviewer's time.

ARRANGE THE POINTS YOU PLAN TO INCLUDE IN YOUR ANSWERS IN LOGICAL ORDER.

Start with a key point and end with a key point. (A key point is one you want the interviewer to pay most attention to, one he or she won't forget.) Those of intermediate interest should go in the middle.

Illustrate each key point with examples, facts and figures obtained from your self-assessment.

YOUR OUTLINE SHOULD HAVE ONLY THE BARE BONES OF WHAT YOU PLAN TO SAY.

Instead of complete sentences, write key words or brief phrases. It helps jog, not clog, your memory.

If you write out the answers word-for-word and then memorize them, you're likely to:
* Forget what you planned to say.
* Lose spontaneity with the result that your answers will appear contrived.
* Lose the flexibility needed to field unexpected questions.

Writing only the key points of each answer:
1. Helps you to be concise.
2. Helps you to remember them.

130

3. Prevents you from straying off course.
4. Makes you appear more logical.
5. Keeps you from putting your foot in your mouth.

It's not only what you say, but how you say it that affects your rating. How you answer gives the interviewer a rough estimate of your intelligence, ability to communicate, and logical mind.

REHEARSE

Knowing what you plan to say is only the preparatory step. Your body has to go through the actual motions so they become ingrained. It's like learning to ice skate. First, you read a book which explains how to do the fancy footwork. But, in order to become a figure skater, you've got to go through the actual motions on ice.

There are three ways to rehearse. Each one reinforces what you learn in the others:

1. Mentally rehearse a successful interview.
2. Role play an interview with someone's help.
3. Go on "live" practice interviews.

MENTAL REHEARSAL: Sit or lie down in a quiet, darkened room where there are no distractions. Visualize an entire interview from the minute you step into the imaginary office until you depart. Repeat these mental rehearsals until you can go through them with ease. Include every important detail:

❀ VISUALIZE HOW YOU APPEAR TO THE "INTERVIEWER":
* Your body language.
* How you greet him/her.
* Your facial expressions.
* The manner in which you depart.
* How you sit, place your arms and legs, make eye contact.

❀ VISUALIZE THE WAY YOU FEEL AND REACT:
* Capable, valuable.

131

* Self-confident, poised.
* Optimistic, upbeat.
* Enthusiastic, eager, interested.
* Patient, calm and polite (especially when stress questions are asked).
* Always emphasizing the positive, even when negative matters are brought up.

❋ VISUALIZE THE CONTENT OF THE INTERVIEW:
* Picture, in your mind, the interviewer as he or she asks questions.
* What you will say.
* How you will say it--Logical, con-cise, relevant, speech, voice tone.

Pay particular attention to the stress questions and visualize yourself responding in a calm, polite, positive manner.

Have fun visualizing how you'll respond when the "interviewer" throws you a fast ball or tries to trip you up some way.

ROLE PLAY AN INTERVIEW

ASK A FRIEND TO HELP YOU. (BETTER YET, ASK A COUNSELOR, FORMER EMP-LOYER OR CO-WORKER.) Give him/her a list of questions you may be asked. Ask your "critic" to take notes on how your speech, voice tone and body language can be improved.

TAPE RECORD THE REHEARSAL FOR LATER STUDY. A videotaped rehearsal helps you to be more objective in admitting your mistakes. The use of videotapes for such purposes is growing among career counselors and outplacement firms.

THE LOCAL COLLEGE CAREER COUNSELING OFFICE MAY HAVE THE EQUIPMENT FOR VIDEOTAPING A PRACTICE INTERVIEW SESSION. Make an appointment with a coun-selor, if possible. Some may also have audio-cassettes which demonstrate proper interview techniques. In many communities, you don't have to be a registered student or an alumnus in order to avail yourself of these services.

THEN PRACTICE BEFORE A MIRROR.

IN YOUR MIND, REPLAY SCENES FROM THE INTERVIEW REHEARSAL WHILE DOING CHORES, WAITING FOR THE BUS, ...

CAUTION: If you rehearse word-for-word as from a prepared script, you'll lose flexibility and a convincing spontaneity. You're more likely be thrown off balance by unexpected deviations from your "script." Actual interviews are bound to differ in varying degrees from what you imagine. By keeping the door open to surprise and variety, you'll become more polished, more professional.

THINGS TO ESPECIALLY WATCH OUT FOR AS YOU REHEARSE THE INTER-VIEW:

* Whether you have a tendency to ramble, especially when answering probing questions.

* Nonverbal and verbal communication which has a negative impact.

WHENEVER POSSIBLE, ACCEPT INTERVIEWS FOR JOBS YOU ARE NOT KEEN ABOUT. It's better to make blunders where it won't matter at first. The more practice you get in live situations, the more focused your answers, and the less nervous you'll be during the really important interview.

When the interview is over ask, "I'd be

grateful if you give me some advice on how to improve my interview skills." Be careful not to let on that you aren't serious about the job; like a blind date you're initially not keen about, you and the employer could turn out to be meant for each other.

IF YOU NEED MORE HELP, THERE ARE WORKSHOPS, SEMINARS AND ADULT EDUCATION COURSES ON HOW TO IMPROVE YOUR JOB INTERVIEW SKILLS. But nothing can take the place of live interview rehearsals.

-10-
HOW TO BOOST
YOUR
SELF-CONFIDENCE

IT'S NATURAL TO HAVE MOMENTS WHEN YOU DOUBT WHETHER ANYONE IS EVER GOING TO HIRE YOU. Most job hunters start out optimistic and confident. After several rejections, reality sets in. If the job market is tight and the person lacks self-confidence to begin with, a full blown case of depression may occur.

YOUR ATTITUDE TOWARD THE INTERVIEW CAN INFLUENCE ITS OUTCOME. "If you don't exhibit faith in yourself, the interviewer is not going to have faith in you," says Josephine Lerro, former director of Human Resources at TempsAmerica.

Before going to an interview ask yourself, "Am I projecting lack of self-confidence or bitterness? Am I going to the interview with preconceived notions that

I'm not going to get hired?"

People who are so full of worries about how they appear to the other person often miss important cues, claims psychologist Jonathan Cheek of Wellesley College. In order to be socially effective, they need to stop focusing on their perceived shortcomings, and switch their attention to the other person. Think of the job interview as a contest of wits rather than a trial, a game that you're going to enjoy rather than lose.

IF THE INTERVIEWER APPEARS COLD, EVEN HOSTILE, it may be an attempt to cover up his/her own nervousness or it may be a deliberate pose to test your poise. It has nothing to do with you.

"Once I was interviewed by a younger woman executive whose every pore seemed to ooze hostility or dislike for me--so I imagined," said a mature professional woman. "Later, I learned she was new on the job and trying hard not to show her nervousness. Although I wasn't hired, the interview was a valuable learning experience. When I called later to thank her and ask for advice on how to improve my interview techniques, she was extremely helpful. She also gave me some valuable job leads."

Some interviewers seem unusually tough because they first screen out traits they don't want in a candidate. Once that is over, they relax and focus on the candidate's positive qualities.

CONCENTRATE ON MAKING THE INTERVIEWER FEEL COMFORTABLE. You may be so preoccupied with your own shyness or nervousness that you overlook the interviewer's situation, whose competence in selecting the best person for the job is on the line. Remind yourself that the two of you are in this pressure cooker together. Your tensions will ease and the interviewer will appreciate your understanding.

THERE ARE PROVEN WAYS TO OVERCOME DEPRESSION AND RAISE YOUR SELF-CONFIDENCE. These range from simple reminders such as those listed above to more complicated and lengthy techniques which have more enduring results. Unless there are deeper psychological or physiological problems, many are self-help techniques.

**IN CASE OF PROLONGED DEPRES-
SION, GET A MEDICAL CHECKUP
FIRST.** An insufficient diet or a
hormonal imbalance may be the cause. A
deficiency of amino acids and vitamin B can
cause depression in susceptible people, says
Dr. Priscilla Slagle, of the University of
California at Los Angeles. Low thyroid or
low adrenal function are also culprits.

**EXERCISE HELPS WARD OFF DE-
PRESSION AND INCREASE YOUR
SENSE OF WELL BEING.** Even
a 15 minute daily, brisk walk brings a significant improvement. Regular exercise increases the body's production of hormones
(beta-endorphines) which act as natural
tranquilizers and help lower blood pressure.

**IF YOU ARE UNEMPLOYED, TRY TO
MAINTAIN A SCHEDULE OF ENJOYABLE
SOCIAL ACTIVITIES.** You'll have more
opportunities to obtain the advice and support of other
people. An active social life reduces depression and
anxiety as well as the body's vulnerability to illness.

Unemployment cuts a person off from many social activities, so force yourself to get out. Plan a weekly or
monthly schedule of interesting and enjoyable things to
do, no matter how trivial. This will give structure to
your day and a sense of direction and control over your
life until you find another job.

**WHY BLAME YOURSELF BECAUSE YOU'VE
LOST YOUR JOB AND CAN'T FIND ANO-
THER AS EASILY AS YOU THOUGHT IT
WOULD BE?** Most workers are dismissed for reasons beyond

They are part of a great evil used by computers to rob people's spirit.
—an American Indian father
(referring to a Social Security number for his child)

their control (e.g., plant closings, mergers, company relocations, job obsolescence, a difficult boss), not because of incompetence. Keep this in mind and your burden of guilt will lighten.

DISPLACING YOUR ANGER ONTO THOSE YOU LOVE DOESN'T IMPROVE YOUR SITUATION. It only reinforces your feelings of unworthiness and misery. Instead, make a plan to improve your situation-- first, by analyzing the errors in your thinking which are self-defeating; second, by correcting them; and third, by making plans for your next job.

PRACTICE POSITIVE HABITS OF THINKING TO MAKE A JOB INTERVIEW SUCCESSFUL. It also improves other areas of your life (e.g., social relationships, marriage, family, career). Moreover, there is medical evidence that it lowers blood pressure and increases the body's resistance to illness (including cancer).

"...If we see things as negative, we are likely to feel negative and behave in a negative way. If we see things as pleasant, we will behave in a positive way and have positive feelings," says psychiatrist Dr. Aaron Beck, of the University of Pennsylvania Medical School.[32]

YOU CAN LEARN A MORE POSITIVE ATTITUDE AND UNLEARN A NEGATIVE ATTITUDE. Basically, cognitive self-therapy is a way of changing the way you habitually view the world and yourself, of erasing negative thought habits from your mind and programming new, more positive ones.

Recent psychological studies show that depressed people have a habit of seeing the world and themselves through cloudy glasses. In one study, two groups of subjects were asked to look into a box in which they saw a series of slides. They had one second to report what they saw on each slide. The depressed group saw "sad faces," "mushroom cloud," "people standing back to back." The nondepressed group reported "happy faces," "a pot of flowers," "two people looking at each other."[31]

OFTEN, THE NEGATIVE VIEW IS NOT BASED ON REALITY. In one study, a group of very shy people were videotaped as they talked to strangers. The tapes were then rated according to how socially skilled they were. In the eyes of the judges, the shy group showed few obvious problems; but the shy people were convinced they had been social flops.

Depressed, shy people have a better memory for their social failures. They've gotten into the habit of attributing any social success to outside factors rather than taking credit for it.

In another study two groups of subjects, one depressed and the other nondepressed, were given rigged assignments in which each would succeed in half and fail in half. When asked to describe their performance, the depressed group recalled the tasks they had failed. The non-depressed group recalled their successes. When asked to give the reasons for their success, the depressed group said luck was the reason; the non-depressed group said skill.

Depressives tend to overgeneralize, say psychologists Ruth Kanfer and Antoinette Zeiss of the University of Arizona. They allow a single failure to make them feel generally worthless. They give up too easily. Even an experience of success gives them no confidence they can do it again.[31]

RECENT STUDIES SHOW THAT PEOPLE WHO LEARN AND PRACTICE SELF-THERAPY SHOW SIGNIFICANT IMPROVEMENT. In one study anxiety levels were measured before and after in two groups of subjects. One group received instructions and practice sessions on self-therapy. The other group received no instructions at all. The instructed group showed a significantly lower stress level compared to the group which did not learn self-therapy skills.

In another study two groups were given an unsolvable task. One group was instructed to repeat over and over to themselves, "There is no logical reason why I should consider myself less competent or worthwhile if I fail at this task." The other group was instructed to repeat, "I'm going to look stupid if I can't solve this simple task." The results showed a significant decrease in anxiety level in the positive self-talk group; none in the other group.[31]

In another experiment, undergraduates who did assignments based on *A New Guide To Rational Living* by Albert Ellis and Robert A. Harper (Wilshire Book Co.) showed a significant decrease in anxiety in social situations and significantly less fear of being evaluated negatively by others.

In fact, the results compared favorably with another study in which a therapist administered the same cognitive therapy skills. In view of this finding, the psychologists claim that many persons can decrease their emotional difficulties and develop greater self-insight by practicing cognitive therapeutic techniques without the aid of a psychotherapist.

(Note, the people involved in the study did not have serious emotional disturbances which required professional help.)

THE MORE YOU GET INVOLVED IN SOCIAL SITUATIONS WHICH CAUSE ANXIETY, THE MORE YOU'LL BE ABLE TO TOLERATE THE DISTRESS SO IT DOES NOT BLOCK YOUR THOUGHTS, writes Dr. Beck (*Anxiety Disorders and Phobias*, Basic Books, 1985). His book gives suggestions for removing faulty beliefs (e.g., the idea that it's shameful to appear anxious in front of others, that other people can detect one's hidden fears and anxieties). People are encouraged to do the actual thing they dread, such as public speaking, until their fear subsides.

IF YOU FOCUS ON YOUR SUCCESSES AND ACHIEVEMENTS, YOU'LL MORE EASILY RECALL OTHER SUCCESSES AND ACHIEVEMENTS. Your mood influences which information comes to mind, claims psychologist Gordon Bower of Stanford University. If you think about a major failure in your life, you'll more easily recall other failures. Think of one event in your life in which you were successful. Dwell on it. Savor it. This makes it easier to recall other successes.

Even reading about positive events will improve your mood, thus making it easier to recall other positive events in your life.

MAKE A LIST OF YOUR SUCCESSES AND ACCOMPLISHMENTS. Identify events since childhood which made you feel good about yourself (e.g., an award, a prize, an accomplished assignment or challenge, compliments).

Analyze each event. What part did you play? How much was due to luck? How much was due to your skill, initiative and ability? Give yourself the credit you deserve.

REWARD YOURSELF EACH TIME YOU ACHIEVE SOMETHING, no matter how small. Gradually, the positive habit of giving yourself credit for success will grow stronger as your negative habit of self blame diminishes.

CONSIDER THE FOREST, NOT ONE TREE. In focusing on one negative experience, you magnify it out of proportion. Instead, analyze the total situation in which it occurred. This helps you find where your thoughts are distorting reality. Eventually, you'll achieve a more positive, objective attitude.

Dr. Aaron Beck had people with a negative outlook do such homework assignments several hours a day. There was a significant improvement. In fact, some studies show cognitive therapy is more effective than drug therapy.

 Nobody is going to come save you; that's your job. Save yourself. If you don't like where you are, get out of there.
— Lillian Hellman

For example, if you dread situations in which you are being evaluated by others, you probably go out of your way to avoid such situations, even to the point of avoiding a career you would otherwise prefer. An objective analysis of the total situation reveals the irrationality of this fear. It helps stop the endless cycle in which fear of failure results in the dreaded poor evaluation which, in turn, reinforces the fear.

ANALYZE THE MOST SELF-DEFEATING THOUGHTS YOU HAVE ABOUT YOURSELF. Ask yourself: Is this based wholly on reality? What can I do to change it? For example:

No one is ever going to hire me.

I'm too (fat, thin, old, young).

It's too late to change.

I lost my job because I don't have what it takes.

I'm going to fall flat on my face at the interview. I'll make a mess of it.

I don't have enough education and it's too late to do anything about it.

All these other people applying for the job are better qualified than I am.

All this new computer technology is beyond me. I'll never be able to adjust to it.

THEN WRITE DOWN ALL THE POSITIVE FACTS AND EVENTS WHICH DISPROVE EACH NEGATIVE THOUGHT. If you can't think of something, it's proof that you're stuck in the groove of negative thinking.

Ask yourself, "What evidence is there for this?" "How much is it due to my own negligence, my own defeatist attitude?"

I didn't try hard enough.

I gave up too soon.

I didn't rehearse the interview.

I didn't come prepared with facts about (the company, my occupation, myself).

I need to take an adult education course to upgrade my skills/knowledge.

❉❉❉❉❉❉❉❉❉❉❉❉❉❉❉❉❉❉❉❉❉❉❉❉❉❉❉❉❉❉❉❉❉❉❉❉

Nobody knows what you want except you. And nobody will be as sorry as you if you don't get it.
—Lillian Hellman

Acknowledge the fact that every day there are people who are older, younger, less educated, fatter, thinner, worse off than you, who make successes of themselves. There are people in their fifth, sixth, even seventh decade of life who get Ph.D.s, change careers, learn a new skill. What's your excuse?

NEXT, MAKE A LIST OF THINGS YOU CAN DO TO IMPROVE YOUR SITUATION. Break up big goals into smaller ones. Then, make a schedule of things to do each day, week and month to achieve your final goal, bit by bit. A series of small successes will reinforce your self-confidence. Here are some suggestions:

Get a part time job.

Go on a diet and exercise regimen.

Buy a good quality suit for job hunting.

Get a more stylish, attractive hairdo or cut.

Become an active volunteer in a local association.

Throw out your old fashioned eyeglasses and get a more fashionable pair.

Enroll in an adult education course to upgrade your skills or learn a new one.

Spend at least two hours a week in the library reading about technological advances in your occupation and industry.

Read Dr. Albert Ellis' *"New Guide to Rational Living"* (Wilshire Book Co.). It is a widely used self-help guide written by a professional for the public.

VISUALIZE A MORE SELF-CONFIDENT, COMPETENT YOU. Visualization is a self-therapy technique. It's based on the theory that you can program your mind to accept a new attitude, even improve a skill, by simply rehearsing it mentally until it becomes firmly imprinted.

Visualization therapy leaves a memory that is almost as good as if you had actually done the action, claims J. Brian Hennessy, a graduate student in neuropsychology at Stanford University. Professional athletes, for example, improve their performance by observing in detail a videotape of a star performer over and over again.[9]

In one experiment, three groups of subjects who suffered from hostility, anxiety and depression were placed in separate, quiet rooms with soothing music. They were asked to lie in a relaxed position with eyes closed. One group was simply told to relax as much as possible. The second group had instructions on muscle feedback relaxation. The third listened to a tape which elicited relaxing images. ("Picture yourself at a warm, quiet seashore.") The visualization group showed the most improvement.[24]

PICTURE YOURSELF AS A COMPETENT EMPLOYEE RATHER THAN "JUST A HOUSEWIFE," if you are a woman returning to work after years of raising a family. "Far too many bring a hang-dog attitude in with them" says a Job Service counselor.

Changing such an attitude should not be difficult if you've done a thorough self-assessment. Take a course on assertiveness training. Contact women's organizations (See the Appendix). Go to the local college or university for information on special programs for women.

HEARING (SELF-TALK) reinforces what you have accomplished by <u>SEEING</u> (e.g., visualizing a successful interview, studying a videotaped interview rehearsal) and <u>DOING</u> (e.g., going on practice "live" interviews, rehearsing an interview, doing a self-assessment).

* Give yourself loud pep talks in front of the mirror or while you are driving or doing chores.

* Before going in say to yourself, "Your organization is going to be proud to have me on board."

* Tape record a diary in which you review your negative thoughts and the ways you can demolish them. Several psychological studies find the regular practice of keeping a written or tape recorded diary significantly improves self-insight and attitude.

You have no idea what a low opinion I have of myself and how little I deserve it.
                                                    —Artie Shaw

One study found that persons who tape recorded or wrote about their troubling emotions daily for a minimum of 15 minutes over a period of time showed as much improvement as those who confide in others. They also made fewer visits to the doctor.

ℛELAXATION TECHNIQUES, such as muscle feedback relaxation, Yoga and Transcendental Meditation, may also reduce anxiety. The biofeedback resulting from just 10 minutes of intense relaxation a day can slow down the heart rate, lower blood pressure and sharpen mental alertness.

However, one researcher reports that it takes at least nine months of practice before a significant improvement in mental health is achieved. Furthermore, some people develop greater anxiety in the early stages of meditation. For these persons, learning to relax the muscles by biofeedback proves more beneficial.

You can find books on relaxation techniques in the library or bookstore. Low cost courses are offered at the Y' and other adult education centers.

IF THE PROBLEMS ARE TOO PERSONAL OR SEVERE, IT'S BEST TO CONSULT A THERAPIST.

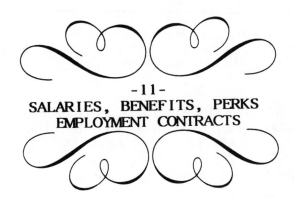

-11-
SALARIES, BENEFITS, PERKS
EMPLOYMENT CONTRACTS

NEVER BRING UP THE MATTER OF PAY EARLY IN THE INTERVIEW. Wait until you have expressed your worth to the employer. Best of all, wait for the interviewer to initiate the subject.

BEFORE THE INTERVIEW, FIND OUT THE LOCAL PAY RANGE FOR THE JOB YOU WANT. It ranges from the lowest entry level pay to the highest pay at the most experienced skilled level.

Be sure to get the local figures rather than the national average for your occupation. The U.S. Department of Labor figures, which are issued periodically for all occupations, do not show state and county variations in pay scales.

If you give a fixed figure which is more than the employer is willing to pay, you won't get the job. If your figure is lower than what you are worth, the employer isn't going to tell you. And, if you give a figure which is way off, the employer will know that you came to the interview unprepared.

By giving the pay range instead of a fixed figure, you'll have room for negotiating a better deal. Say something to this effect: "I understand the local pay range for this job is between --- and ---." Then wait for the interviewer to make an offer.

IF YOU HAVEN'T BEEN ABLE TO LEARN WHAT THE PAY RANGE IS, it's better to ask, "What is the pay <u>range</u> for the job in this community?" instead of asking "What does the job pay?" By asking for the pay range, you will have room to negotiate a higher figure.

IT'S EASIER TO CONVINCE AN EMPLOYER THAT YOU ARE WORTH MORE THAN THE INITIAL OFFER IF YOU'VE DONE A SELF-ASSESSMENT. Give the facts and figures which show how you helped your previous employers increase productivity (e.g., time saved, percentage reduction in defective goods, dollar increase in sales, rate of decline in absenteeism in your department). Also mention salary increases.

NEGOTIATE EVEN IF THE EMPLOYER MAKES A FLAT OFFER rather than ask what salary you expect. According to some placement counselors, a few hundred dollars more a year won't make much difference to the company, but it might meet a mortgage payment for you. The only valid criterion should be that you are worth the increase.

IF THIS DOESN'T WORK, ASK IF THERE WILL BE AN EARLY EVALUATION OF YOUR JOB PERFORMANCE. Since you are an unknown quantity, the employer may want to test your performance during a trial period before raising your pay to the level you deserve. If your skills are in demand, you have a bargaining chip in that there's the danger of losing you to a more generous employer.

A manufacturer's representative whose last job paid $40,000 found a job after many months of searching. The starting salary was $30,000. Three months later she got an unexpected raise of $5,000.

IF THE SALARY OFFERED IS LOWER THAN YOU EXPECT:

Don't be too shy to ask, "Is that figure negotiable?"

Some employers offer less during a trial period in which a new worker's performance is evaluated. Inquire about this.

In times of stiff competition and a surplus labor pool, many employers lower their starting salaries. They also take other cost-cutting measures, such as increasing the length of time between salary reviews, reducing pay raises, scaling back hiring plans and forcing employees to take pay cuts. This trend began in 1983-84. According to *The Wall Street Journal*, if it continues, people with average skills who made $30,000 yearly will be earning $6,000 before long.

THE JOB APPLICATION FORM WILL ASK YOU TO WRITE THE SALARY YOU EXPECT. It's safer to write "negotiable" and discuss the matter during the interview than to give a precise figure or leave it blank.

IF, BEFORE GIVING YOU THE DETAILS OF THE JOB, THE INTERVIEWER ASKS WHAT PAY YOU EXPECT, say you need more information about your responsibilities, the work conditions, advancement opportunities and company paid benefits.

IF YOU ARE HIGHLY SKILLED AND THE DEMAND FOR YOUR SKILLS IS GREATER THAN THE SUPPLY, get off your knees and ask for what you are worth. Otherwise, the employer will think you're not as good as you really are. Employers will agree to almost anything if they want you badly enough.

DON'T BE AFRAID TO SAY, "I DON'T THINK THE SALARY YOU'RE OFFERING REFLECTS

MY SKILLS AND EXPERIENCE." However, learn beforehand the competition you're up against so you won't jeopardize your chances of being chosen. If you don't assert yourself on the issue of pay, the employer may think you lack drive and ambition, or that you aren't worth more.

APPLICANTS NEAR RETIREMENT AGE should consider where they are starting from, how many years they have left to give to the company and the amount of competition for the job. Whatever the situation, they should be aware the employer will try to get them as cheaply as possible.

According to a Job Service counselor, many older applicants price themselves out of a job because they fail to be realistic about the job market. They may be competing with younger workers who are willing to accept less and have more up-to-date skills and knowledge.

NEVER TRY TO TRICK AN EMPLOYER INTO OFFERING A HIGHER SALARY BY LYING ABOUT YOUR PREVIOUS ONE.

IF YOU CANNOT CONVINCE THE EMPLOYER TO OFFER MORE, TRY TO NEGOTIATE A BETTER BENEFITS PACKAGE.

A RELATIVELY LOW PAY OFFER PLUS A GOOD BENEFITS PACKAGE WITH FREQUENT SALARY REVIEWS IS WORTH MORE IN THE LONG RUN. It may include company paid health and life insurance, more paid vacation and sick days, free tuition, job training and frequent performance evaluations.

According to Marilyn Moats Kennedy, author of *Salary Strategies* (Rawson Associates, 1982), such benefits cost an employer from 25% to 45% of a worker's pay. This adds up to an additional $5,000 to $9,000 on a $20,000 yearly salary.

FIND OUT THE STANDARD NUMBER OF PAID VACATION, HOLIDAY AND SICK DAYS IN THE OCCUPATION AND INDUSTRY.

ALSO, LEARN WHAT OTHER BENEFITS AND PERKS YOU CAN REASONABLY EXPECT.

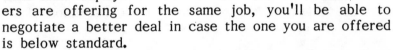

Some employers offer two to three times the standard pension benefits. Some offer no pension benefits at all for the type of job you want.

If you know what other employers are offering for the same job, you'll be able to negotiate a better deal in case the one you are offered is below standard.

If the benefits offer is substandard, don't be afraid to ask for an explanation. (A small, newly established business may not be able to afford as much health and hospitalization benefits. In 1984-85 only 31% of workers in the smallest firms had both health insurance and retirement benefits, compared with 91% of workers in big companies, reports the Small Business Association.)

IT HELPS TO KNOW THE ADDITIONAL PERKS EMPLOYERS OFFER.

Merit pay
Paid tuition
Profit sharing
Paid sabbaticals
Dental care plan
Free legal advice
Free home computer

Low interest loans
Subsidized cafeteria
Extra life insurance
Use of a company car
Flexible working hours
Paid health club membership
Paid attendance at conventions, trade shows & conferences

GENERALLY, THE HIGHER UP THE CAREER LADDER, THE GREATER THE NUMBER AND QUALITY OF PERKS WHICH CAN BE NEGOTIATED. Some of these can be exotic. For example, a Fortune 500 corporation in 1984 offered its top executives a week's stay at a Swiss rejuvenation clinic, complete with youth cell injections.

At lower occupational levels the number of people applying for jobs is generally greater than the number of openings. If you're at this level, know what you can reasonably expect so you won't make exorbitant requests which will knock you out of the game.

BECAUSE SMALL COMPANIES GENERALLY CANNOT AFFORD TO PAY THE SAME SALARY LEVELS AS LARGE ONES, IT MAY BE EASIER TO NEGOTIATE FOR CERTAIN BENEFITS.

Caution: Since the chances of a small company failing are much higher, think twice about accepting a benefit offer which pays off in the future (i.e., stock shares).

(See chapters two and three for a discussion of the advantages of working for a small company.)

PERSONS NEAR RETIREMENT AGE who may not be able to find a job paying the salary they are worth should try for a better benefits deal. The employer is getting the best of the bargain either way.

ASK FOR FULL DETAILS ON CERTAIN BENE-FITS. Don't expect the interviewer to volunteer all the information you need to know. For example:

If the job involves traveling a lot, you should be concerned about travel and accident insurance.

If you plan to stay with the company a long time, you'll want to know about profit sharing and pension benefits.

Company paid medical plans vary greatly in the a-mount of coverage provided.

Don't take up too much of the employer's time with minute details about medical and pension plans. The personnel department is the best source for this infor-mation.

IF YOU ARE OFFERED THE JOB BUT YOU DON'T HAVE THE INFORMATION NEEDED TO COMPARE THE BENEFITS OFFER WITH THE INDUSTRY STANDARD, say you are highly interested but need to know the the income value of the total package. Play it by ear.

EMPLOYMENT CONTRACTS:

An employment contract is a written agreement between an employer and an about-to-be-hired employee which provides certain assurances for each. The employer has a guarantee that the worker will not quit within a stated period of time, and the worker is assured of one or more of the following:

He/She will not be dismissed on grounds other than clearly specified job performance standards.

The salary and benefits discussed during the interview will be granted.

In case of dismissal, certain sweeteners will be given to help tide the worker over.

Employment contracts have generally been given to persons at the top rungs of a career ladder (in 1984-85, those earning $75,000 or more). Lately, however, as a result of mass layoffs at the middle management and professional levels, persons earning less are asking for, and getting, contracts.

There are also situations where highly skilled persons who accept unusual assignments at a lower pay are given a contract. For example, in 1980 a sociologist was offered a research position at a university, at a measly $18,000 a year. She was handed a formal letter which stated the salary, starting date, her major responsibilities and the person to whom she was to report. The letter was vague about continuing employment after com-

pletion of the project, and there was no mention of medical insurance, vacation time and other aspects of the job which had been discussed at the interview. Five months later it became clear that:

She had to pay for her own medical insurance.

State funds to continue the project beyond the stated duration of employment would not be forthcoming, and she would be out of a job.

The "one month" vacation had shrunk to two weeks.

Supplies which were necessary to do professional work were interminably late in coming, if at all.

In fact, she didn't even have an office. She had to share a desk top in a small, cramped office, with her secretary's typewriter clattering away in her ears.

The moral of this true story is:

BE SURE YOU HAVE ALL THE IMPORTANT DETAILS OF THE EMPLOYMENT AGREEMENT IN WRITING. These might include any of the following:

* Bonuses
* Vacation time
* Your job title
* Job Description
* Salary agreed upon
* Incentives for superior work
* Fringe benefits, such as stock options
* The specific reasons for which you can be dismissed
* The amount and duration of severance pay in the event of job loss due to a merger or other reason which has nothing to do with your performance
* In case the new job is in another community, relocation expenses, transportation expenses for job hunting, even an agreement to make up some of the difference between the old and new mortgages (Be sure it includes the length of time such assistance will be granted.)

THE MORE COMPLEX THE CONTRACT and the higher the stakes involved, the more important it is to have a lawyer look it over before you sign it.

Technological genius is one of the glories of mankind. It has . . . made it possible via satellite for comfortable Americans to watch Ethiopians starve. —Tom Wicker, "The Ignorant Genius"

NEVER SIGN A CONTRACT WHICH HAS THE REASONS FOR WHICH YOU CAN BE DIS-MISSED STATED IN AMBIGUOUS TERMS (e.g., "incompetence," "neglect of duty," "for cause"). The employer can use these as an excuse to get rid of you simply because he/she doesn't like your looks or politics. The standards of poor performance must be spelled out clearly.

PROCEED WITH CAUTION. Generally, companies aren't keen about contracts for employees below the top levels. A few companies have a no-contract policy even at the vice-presidential level.

Only after an offer is made and the terms of employment have been discussed should you ask for a confirming letter.

If you meet with resistance, don't push it. Point out the mutual advantages of a contract.

If that doesn't work, drop the matter.

AVOID USING ADVERSARY TERMS, such as "I" vs. "You," advises John Stickney (MONEY, December 1984). Using "we" implies you are already a member of the team.

MOST JOBS DON'T CALL FOR A WRITTEN AGREEMENT. THOSE THAT DO INCLUDE:

Work on a specific project which will eventually be completed.

Occupations requiring professional or special skills and talents which make it difficult for a person to find another job easily (e.g., chief executive officers, professors, entertainers).

Assignments which require "rescuing" a company or project from the brink of failure.

WHERE TO FIND MORE DETAILED IN-FORMATION ON SALARIES, BENEFITS AND PERKS:

Read the help wanted ads to see what other employers are offering. (Don't rely on the glitteringly high salaries advertised by for-profit employment agencies.)

Call the Job Service office for advice.

Use your personal contacts who are in the same occupation or industry.

Go to the public library and look up the trade or professional association for your occupation and industry in Gale's *Encyclopedia of Associations*. These associations do annual salary surveys for their members. Write or call for information.

Ask the reference librarian to help you locate salary surveys made by private and public organizations.

Contact your state's department of labor. It should have information on local or area wages.

The placement office of the local school or college may have the information you want. If not, they can refer you to another source.

For information on standard benefits in the industry, write to: The Employee Benefit Research Institute, 2121 K Street NW, Suite 860, Washington, D.C. 20037.

Read one of the suggested books in the Appendix.

12

THE JOB APPLICATION FORM
JOB REFERENCES

THE JOB APPLICATION IS A LEGAL DOCUMENT FOR THE COMPANY'S RECORDS. Generally, it asks for the following information:

Education: high school class ranking, college major, favorite subject, extra-curricular activities, offices held, honors, what you liked most/least about school, portion of college expenses earned, future education plans, etc.

Experience

Leisure Activities: membership in social, civic and professional associations; hobbies and interests; reading preferences; what you like to do on vacations.

Goals: future plans, highlights of your past experience, major accomplishments.

Health Status, including height and weight. (If it asks "any physical disabilities?," the law states you are not required to list any problem which does not interfere with your job performance.)

Family: marital status, number and ages of children, child care arrangements.

GIVING FALSE INFORMATION ON A LEGAL DOCUMENT CAN GET YOU INTO HOT WATER. Soon after you are hired, you may be asked to submit proof of age for insurance purposes or undergo medical screening for drug or alcohol abuse. A lie can cost you the job. Nowadays more employers are investigating the background of prospective employees, and modern communication methods make it easier to detect a falsehood.

For entry level jobs, employers may only verify recent employment: dates, title, pay, reliability and work performance. But for certain jobs (those paying a high salary, involving sensitive matters, or requiring critical skills) some employers hire investigating agencies to check the applicant's background as far back as ten years.

THE LAW PROHIBITS THE APPLICATION FROM ASKING FOR YOUR BIRTH DATE, RELIGION, NATIONALITY AND RACE. If it If it does, you may leave the question blank.

IT IS LEGAL, HOWEVER, TO ASK FOR YOUR APPROXIMATE AGE, as in "Fill in the blank next to your age range (e.g., 50 to 60)." If you leave it blank, it might be viewed as carelessness.

FOR GRADUATION DATES (OR SCHOOLING COMPLETED), many experts advise applicants over 45 to write only the most recent dates and ignore the earlier ones (high school and elementary attendance). Others say you must include all dates since this is not an illegal question.

ONE OF THE MOST IMPORTANT QUESTIONS IS WHY YOU WANT TO WORK FOR THE COMPANY. Stress your skills and other qualities which will be assets to the firm. Avoid focusing on your own needs. (e.g., "I like the pay," or "It's

---

I like the man who, whenever he encountered the question "race?" in an application, answered simply with the word "human."
—Paul Tabori,"The Natural Science of Stupidity"

158

close to my home.")

THE ACCURACY, THOROUGHNESS, LEGIBILITY AND NEATNESS WITH WHICH YOU ANSWER THE QUESTIONS WILL ALSO BE RATED. Be sure to:

Write Legibly: If your handwriting is awful, ask to use the office typewriter or take the form home to type. Use a pen instead of pencil, and make it readable.

Answer Every Question: zip code, telephone area code, etc. Leaving some questions blank may be viewed as carelessness or evasiveness. Answer each question as completely as space permits. If some of the questions do not apply to you (e.g., military experience) write "None" or "Does not apply." Use your resume to jog your memory.

Follow Every Instruction: If it says, "Please print," don't write in cursive style.

If it asks "Expected Salary," don't write "anything" or give a precise figure. Write "Negotiable" or "Open" and you'll appear more business-like.

Make It Neat: Do not scratch out mistakes or mess it up in any other way.

EMPLOYERS ALSO USE THE APPLICATION FORM TO GET INFORMATION ON YOUR OVERALL COMPATIBILITY WITH THE JOB AND THE ORGANIZATION. Information you give which reveals your interests, attitudes and personality can tip the balance for or against you.

THE APPLICATION MAY BE ANALYZED FOR CERTAIN PERSONALITY TRAITS. It may be used as a handwriting sample which is analyzed by a graphologist for personality traits which are required for the job (e.g., self-confidence, aggressiveness, introversion and creativity). (You may be asked for an additional handwriting sample.) Handwriting is seen as a form of "body language" which reveals a candidate's underlying attitudes and personality characteristics. (Grapholoanalysis cannot detect age, sex or race.)

AVOID LISTING ACTIVITIES IN ORGANIZATIONS WHOSE POLITICAL AND SOCIAL FOCUS may prejudice the employer against you (e.g., ethnic, National Rifle Association, Gay Rights, John Birch Society, Ku Klux Klan, Young Republicans or Democrats, W.O.W., N.O.W. and Gray Panthers).

Do list neutral associations: professional, civic and sports.

Any so-called negative information (your beliefs regarding politics, race, sex, religion or other social topics) can override positive information (your abilities, intelligence, experience).

JOB REFERENCES

THE BEST PERSONS TO USE AS REFERENCES ARE THOSE WHO CAN DESCRIBE YOUR QUALIFICATIONS FOR THE JOB IN DETAIL (e.g., former employers, co-workers, teachers, professors, members of associations in which you are active and organizations in which you worked as a volunteer.) Employers generally ignore relatives and friends unless these persons have observed your job performance and social relations skills.

GET PERMISSION BEFORE USING SOMEONE'S NAME AS A REFERENCE. Do this even if you know the person well. Better no reference at all than a lukewarm or negative one.

IF A VALUABLE CONTACT PERSON IS SO BUSY THAT HE/SHE IS LIKELY TO SAY "SORRY, I HAVE NO TIME," ask if it would be more convenient to have the employer phone instead of writing for information.

This is the 35th anniversary of my 39th birthday.
—Ronald Reagan on his 74th birthday

A REQUEST FOR A REFERENCE THAT IS MADE IN PERSON IS LESS LIKELY TO BE REFUSED. If that's impossible, use the telephone; then follow up with a brief letter.

MAKE SURE YOU HAVE THE CORRECT NAME, SPELLING, CURRENT ADDRESS AND PHONE NUMBER. Employers are turned off when a letter is returned from the post office because of an applicant's careless error. If a valued contact person sees his/her name misspelled, how seriously do you think your request for a good recommendation will be taken?

GIVE THE CONTACT PERSON A COPY OF YOUR RESUME AND DETAILED INFORMATION ON THE JOB YOU ARE APPLYING FOR. This makes it easier to describe your qualifications accurately and give information an employer needs. Make sure the contact person knows why you are the best person for the job.

IF A VALUED CONTACT PERSON IS OFTEN OUT OF TOWN, TRY TO GET THE PHONE NUMBERS AND SCHEDULE WHERE HE/SHE CAN BE REACHED. Give this to the employer. Should the employer call when that person is away, it could be the fatal flaw in your application for a job where there is much competition.

IF YOU DON'T WANT YOUR PRESENT EMPLOYER TO BE CONTACTED FOR FEAR OF JEOPARDIZING YOUR JOB, SAY SO. The interviewer will understand. Say you will be happy to allow a contact to be made if you have reasonable assurance the job is yours.

The closest some of us will ever come to perfection is when we are filling out a job application.
—Arnold H. Glasow

13

"WHY WERE YOU DISMISSED?" & OTHER EMBARRASSING QUESTIONS

ONG GAPS BETWEEN JOBS MUST BE EX-PLAINED, or the interviewer may wonder if you've been incapacitated in some way. You must have done something constructive such as free-lance carpentry, typing, computer programming, word processing, or writing. Did you work part time, attend adult education classes, start a home business?

If you can't think of anything, you can always say, "I attended to personal matters."

JOB HOPPING IS NO LONGER A KISS OF DEATH. On the average, people change jobs 7 times and careers 3 times during their lives, reported *Business Week* in 1984. These figures will rise dramatically in the coming years. There is a big bulge of baby boomers who are competing for fewer and fewer jobs at the middle management level. Many will drop out of the fast track to seek new careers or become entrepreneurs.

Employees who put in 15 or more years with the same company used to be valued as loyal and dependable. Not anymore. In times of rapid change and new challenges, employers don't want people who follow orders blindly, who fail to grow as a result of doing the same, narrow responsibilities year after year.

Furthermore, the old belief that loyalty to the boss will be rewarded with job security is dying out as a result of the recent, drastic cuts in clerical and middle management jobs.

ADISMISSAL DOESN'T MEAN A PERSON IS FINISHED NOWADAYS. IT'S HAPPENING MORE OFTEN AND TO THE BEST OF US. For many people, it's a blessing in disguise. It forces them to go on to better things, to do the kind of work they have always dreamed of doing.

Lee Iacocca was fired after 30 years of devoted service to the Ford Motor Company. It was one of the best things that could have happened. It forced him to accept a job few executives wanted, that of saving the Chrysler Corporation from bankruptcy. His astounding success made him a national hero.

TRY TO NEGOTIATE A SEVERANCE DEAL. More employers are offering "sweeteners" to dismissed workers in an effort to avoid lawsuits and maintain good community relations. Severance benefits have, until recently, been given only to upper management and executive level employees. Now clerical and blue collar victims of mass dismissals are receiving some of the following:
* Mortgage assistance
* Use of company's address
* Temporary continuation of pay
* Payment for lost pension rights
* Use of an office and secretarial help
* Temporary continuation of health insurance
* Continued use of title for job hunting purposes
* Outplacement services; payment for career counseling and employment agency fees

Your chances of getting a good severance deal increase if the following conditions prevail:
* You're at a high level in the company.
* You have been with the company for years.

* You were dismissed for political or economic reasons.

* Your occupation is one in which finding another job will take longer (e.g., a professional or top management job, an occupation which is threatened with obsolescence).

* You are calm and objective during the discussion. You rely on logic and avoid making demands.

WORRIED THAT A FORMER EMPLOYER WILL GIVE YOU A POOR REFERENCE? Relax, most employers give as little negative information as possible. One reason is fear of a defamation lawsuit. Another is the effect on their reputation as responsible employers. The best job applicants will avoid them.

FIND OUT IF YOUR STATE HAS A LAW RESTRICTING EMPLOYERS' RIGHTS TO DISCLOSE INFORMATION ABOUT EMPLOYEES. If so, you are entitled to read your employment record and register a rebuttal. In 1984, 33 states had such a law. Contact the U.S. Department of Labor or your state's department of labor/employment.

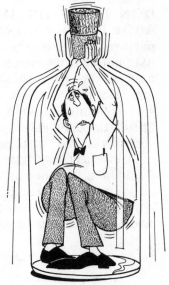

IF THERE IS EVIDENCE THAT A FORMER EMPLOYER IS BLACK-BALLING YOU:

♣ Try to salvage the situation. (See below.)

♣ See a lawyer about filing a defamation suit. Or, hire a labor relations attorney. This can be an expensive and lengthy procedure, but it has worked for discharged executives.

♣ Hire a reputable investigating service to provide certification of your credentials which you'll use to convince potential employers. In 1985, the costs of such investigating ranged from $50 to $400.

Look in the *Yellow Pages* or contact the public library for the names and addresses of reputable services in your area. Be sure to check their reputation before you sign any contract.

tHERE ARE SUBTLE WAYS TO EXPLAIN WHY YOU QUIT OR WERE FIRED WHICH WON'T MAKE YOU APPEAR TO BE A DIFFICULT PERSON. The interviewer will get the message and appreciate your diplomacy if you say something to this effect:

"I had gone as far as I could in the company."

"I quit in order to find a job where I can develop further in my career."

"The conditions for doing my work to the best of my ability were not available."

"I want more opportunity to develop my skills and knowledge."

BEGIN BY SAYING SOMETHING FAVORABLE ABOUT THE JOB AND THE COMPANY. For example, "I enjoyed my coworkers and the supervisor was a nice person," or something to that effect.

DON'T SAY OR IMPLY ANYTHING NEGATIVE ABOUT YOUR FORMER EMPLOYER. If your departure was due to a personality conflict, do not malign that person. The interviewer will assume the same thing will occur in the new job. Do this even if the supervisor or boss was at fault. It shows a lack of professionalism to denigrate previous employers. It also marks you as a person who bears grudges.

You might say something like this: "My supervisor and I had a difference of opinion which couldn't be reconciled and so we agreed that it would be best if I leave." That's much better than saying, "That S.O.B. made my life miserable."

A gossip is one who talks to you about others; a bore is one who talks to you about himself; and a brilliant conversationalist is one who talks to you about yourself.
— Lisa Kirk

AVOID DISPLAYING NEGATIVE FEELINGS WITH YOUR BODY "LANGUAGE." This can be a dead give-away of your true feelings, even as you say flattering things about your previous employer.

IF YOU MUST DESCRIBE NEGATIVE ASPECTS OF YOUR PREVIOUS EMPLOYMENT, BE NEUTRAL ABOUT IT. Instead of saying, "The job was a bore. There were few challenges," you might say, "There was little opportunity to do my best work under the prevailing conditions."

Instead of saying, "My supervisor was a paranoid bastard. Everyone hated him," you might say, "The supervisor was relatively inexperienced and new on the job." Or, "He was the boss's nephew. I saw no opportunity for advancement."

SOME COMPANIES ARE MORE LIKELY TO ACCEPT AN EXPLANATION WHICH STRESSES YOUR CREATIVE NATURE. More often than not, it's the creative people who get into hot water. They're more apt to make mistakes because they are willing to try something new in an effort to do things better. If this was your problem, take heart. Small, entrepreneurial companies value this type of employee. Many high-tech firms actually encourage creative employees to risk falling on their faces.

BE AS HONEST AND OBJECTIVE AS POSSIBLE. If it was a matter of performance and you were responsible for the dismissal, you can say something like this: "I was in the wrong job. I've since done a self-assessment and I know I'm better suited for this one." Then point out how your qualifications are more relevant to this job opening.

"There were certain problems at the time which influenced my performance. I've learned from the experience, and I know darned well that I won't let it happen again, because this job means a lot to me."

John C., a computer technician, was fired at a time his life was falling apart. His wife had left him and their two sons in order to "find herself." This adversely affected his relations with his boss and coworkers. Despite the high demand for his skills, he was turned down repeatedly because each time his former employer was contacted, negative information was given.

John's mistake was trying to hide a reality which eventually came to light. It made him appear untrustworthy. The situation took a brighter turn when he decided to tell the truth about the reasons for his dismissal.

He pointed to his prior excellent work record. He assured the interviewer that the home situation had improved since he was granted custody of the boys. "Iron becomes steel when it's been tempered with fire," he said. He got the job and now he is more careful about letter personal problems interfere with his work.

YOU CAN STATE THE REAL REASON FOR THE MISUNDERSTANDING, AS LONG AS YOU DON'T DISPLAY A SOUR GRAPES ATTITUDE. Mainly, it's your personality which is under scrutiny in this situation, not the fact of a dismissal. How you handle it makes all the difference in the world.

Be sure to support your view with positive evidence: "My supervisor was new on the job and he didn't have the time to arrange the conditions which were necessary for me to do the job well. Would you like to hear what I accomplished, despite that?"

REASSURE THE INTERVIEWER THAT YOU ARE NOT A POOR RISK. Mention your past achievements and good references. Say something like this, "Let me tell you what I achieved and what I learned on the job." The interviewer is bound to be impressed with your humility, honesty, desire to improve and the even-handed way you have answered the question.

Mention other situations in which you displayed excellent teamwork and good relationships with peers and persons in authority: a job, volunteer work, sports, school.

Progress is impossible without change, and those who cannot change their minds cannot change anything.
— George Bernard Shaw

THERE ARE ALWAYS POSITIVE ASPECTS TO A NEGATIVE SITUATION. MOST PEOPLE LEARN FROM THEM. LOOK FOR THEM.

IF YOU QUIT YOU LAST JOB BECAUSE YOUR CONSCIENCE WOULDN'T PERMIT YOU TO CHEAT BY JOB HUNTING ON COMPANY TIME, SAY SO. Such honesty appears to be rare these days of musical chairs in job hunting. The interviewer may be so flabbergasted that you'll be offered a job on the spot.

IF YOUR DEPARTURE WAS NOT CORDIAL, IT MAY STILL BE POSSIBLE TO GET YOUR FORMER BOSS TO REMEMBER YOU KINDLY. Time heals all wounds. Wait until things cool off before making an attempt to see him/her. In the meantime, a review of your personal assets and past achievements will boost your ego.

Swallow your pride and thank the employer for giving you the opportunity to work for the organization. It's better to do this in person than over the phone. If the boss refuses to see you, write a brief letter.

Get the boss in the mood to say "Yes" before you make any request. Bring up points on which there can be no disagreement about your best qualities as an employee.

"When there were rush deadlines to meet, who could be relied upon to volunteer to work overtime, including weekends?"

"Do you recall that I was one of the few who showed up for work the day after New Years?"

"Would you say my attendance been above average?"

"Have I ever had an accident on the job?"

Remind the boss of your best achievements while you were an employee. It's possible he/she has overlooked them in anger.

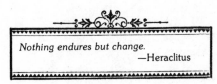

Nothing endures but change.
                                            —Heraclitus

Ask for advice on how to make your work performance even better. Your humility and desire to improve is bound to make a positive impression. Also, you may learn something valuable to help in your next interview.

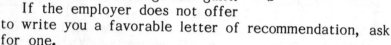

Ask how to clear the record so you won't have difficulty finding another job. Most employers are willing to help dismissed workers. It's good for their reputation and it eases their feelings of guilt.

If the employer does not offer to write you a favorable letter of recommendation, ask for one.

Never imply the boss was wrong to dismiss you. Avoid pouring salt into the wound. Instead of reinforcing the feelings of guilt, it may convince him/her the decision was right.

If the boss gets angry, don't raise your voice, argue, curse or threaten to sue. Wait until he/she releases the pent up feelings. After he calms down, say what you have to say. Rely on logic and gentle persuasion instead of demands or threats.

Get off your knees and speak as a respectful equal. Don't ask for forgiveness or special favors.

This advice, like so many others, needs qualification. The degree of finesse required to follow it through depends on the personalities involved and the situation which led to the unpleasantness. For some people, it could backfire. Play it by ear.

NOW IS THE TIME TO BRING UP IN-FORMATION WHICH IS NOT IN THE RESUME. Don't waste the interviewer's time by repeating what's in the resume except to emphasize an important point.

IF YOU ARE OFFERED A JOB THAT IS LESS THAN WHAT YOU HOPED FOR but is a stepping stone in that direction, don't reject it out-right. Say you're interested in proving your value to the company. Then ask about the possibilities of increasing your responsibilities in the near future.

Don't expect to be viewed as management material just because you were president of the P.T.A. or have a Ph.D. People in the business world are more impressed by "hands on" experience which shows concrete results in the form of increased profit. They first want to test your competence before promoting you to a position that is commensurate with your abilities.

BE PREPARED TO ANSWER QUESTIONS ON THE FOLLOWING: Long periods of unemployment, why you quit or were dismissed from a job and, especially if you are near retirement age, physical disabilities which might interfere with your ability to do the job.

SHOW ENTHUSIASM ABOUT THE JOB AND THE ORGANIZATION.

A candidate who is looking for a job of any kind raises the suspicion that nobody else wants to hire him or her. It's also a fatal mistake to ask questions about vacation and fringe benefits before there is a clear indication of an offer.

INFORMATION YOU GIVE SHOULD BE RELEVANT TO THE QUESTIONS ASKED AND THE PURPOSE OF THE INTERVIEW.

Omit personal matters and other irrelevancies such as the difficulty you had getting there. The interviewer is not interested in your problems or your life story, no matter how fascinating these are to you.

DON'T MAKE EXCUSES FOR YOUR LACK OF PREPARATION.

(e.g., "I didn't have time to find out what the salary range for this job is," or "I don't know about other job categories in this organization that I could fill five years from now.") Instead, reverse the interviewer's question with one of your own: "Which jobs in this company can a person with my abilities and ambition aspire to?"

ADMIT THAT YOU DON'T KNOW THE ANSWER TO A FACTUAL QUESTION, BUT SAY YOU'LL FIND OUT SOON.

The interviewer won't be impressed by your attempts at bluffing.

DISPLAY YOUR SENSE OF HUMOR WITH WIT RATHER THAN JOKES.

Wit appeals to the interviewer's intelligence whereas a joke forces him

172

or her to put the brakes on the interview in order to listen and laugh, no matter how bad your joke is. This also upsets the normal balance of power.

NEVER REVEAL THE OFFICE POLITICS IN YOUR FORMER PLACE OF EMPLOYMENT. It stigmatizes you as a dangerous person to have around.

DEMONSTRATE A WILLINGNESS AND ABILITY TO DO ANYTHING THE JOB REQUIRES (within reason, of course).

IF YOU ARE ASKED ABOUT A SPECIFIC SKILL OR KNOWLEDGE YOU NEED TO UPDATE, don't fake it (unless it's something you can acquire quickly). Blunt honesty won't do you much good either (e.g., "I'm not good at that.") It's better to give an answer which indicates your capacity for further growth. (e.g., "As a matter of fact, I'm planning to take courses in that area because I'm very interested and hope to become more expert in it.")

INSTEAD OF FOCUSING ON YOUR OWN NEEDS, point out how your experience and abilities will benefit the employer.

BEFORE REPLYING, LISTEN CAREFULLY AND KNOW EXACTLY WHAT INFORMATION IS RE-QUESTED. The interviewer expects you to pause while you organize your thoughts according to these guidelines:

- ♣ What you want
- ♣ The employer's needs
- ♣ The demands of the job
- ♣ The employer's hiring criteria
- ♣ the "personality" requirements of the job and the organization

IF YOU HAVEN'T WORKED IN MANY YEARS, OR IF IT'S YOUR FIRST JOB, the employer will be concerned about your ability to adapt quickly to the workplace environment. Reassure him or her by citing any part-time employment and/or extra-curricular and voluntary activities which show you understand the importance of:

- ♣ Teamwork
- ♣ Meeting deadlines
- ♣ Sticking to a schedule
- ♣ Dealing with office politics
- ♣ Presenting the desired "image"

tHE OLDER YOU ARE THE MORE IMPOR-TANT TO GIVE ASSURANCE THAT YOUR ENERGY LEVEL IS UP TO THE DEMANDS OF THE JOB. If you had an excellent attendance record in your previous job, if you are in reasonably good health, if you engage in sports activities regularly, say so. If you walk a mile each day to buy the newspaper or go out dancing on weekends, let the interviewer know. Cite recent medical reports that show older Americans today have more stamina and energy than those of a generation ago.

MENTION RECENT ACTIVITIES WHICH DEMONSTRATE YOUR OPENNESS TO CHANGE AND ABILITY TO ADAPT (e.g., travel, volunteer work, preparations for a career change, adult education courses taken, creative projects completed.) This is especially important if you are 45 or over. Make it clear that while you've had many life experiences, you are always willing to learn something new.

AVOID GIVING THE IMPRESSION OF "TALKING DOWN," of being condescending or overbearing. Try to allay any discomfort a much younger interviewer may have about your seniority. Tone down the assertiveness that all job applicants are advised to demonstrate, but without giving the appearance of passivity.

Though the interviewer may appear as a child to you, remind yourself that he/she probably has more up-to-date information than you have about the job and industry.

Cite examples of your good teamwork skills. Inform the interviewer of the many studies which show older workers have a better attitude toward the boss, that they are more willing to carry out orders. (Be careful not to overdo the latter or you may appear to be in need of too much supervision.)

Amy Glickman writes of the clash that can occur between an older woman employee and a young female boss. Whereas with young coworkers the older woman may show an irritating deferential attitude, she may display a maternal attitude toward her boss which can be infuriating. "You sort of want to pick up after them and wipe their noses," said a 46 year old software specialist who admits "freaking out" when she began working with younger people. [36]

The older woman must contend with the stereotype that she is difficult to manage, that she tends to resist directives and get upset when a young manager treats her as an employee instead of a sister.

IF THE INTERVIEWER DOESN'T BRING UP THE SUBJECT OF AGE, THERE IS NO REASON WHY YOU SHOULD. If the matter is brought up, convey a sense of pride in your years of achievement and learning. (Remember, it's illegal for the interviewer to ask questions about your age.)

The hardest thing about climbing the ladder of success is to get through the crowd at the bottom.

— Anonymous

IF YOU DON'T UNDERSTAND OR HEAR A QUESTION CLEARLY, the way to avoid giving the impression of being hard of hearing is to ask for clarification instead of mumbling or saying something inappropriate. Say something to this effect, "The way I define your question is....Is that how you define it?" That's much better than saying, "I didn't hear you. Will you please repeat the question."

DON'T MENTION ANY HEALTH PROBLEM WHICH DOES NOT INTERFERE WITH YOUR ABILITY TO DO THE JOB. On the other hand, if you have a chronic problem which will affect your performance, you shouldn't be applying for that job. There are other opportunities and work situations where you'll be more comfortable and happy.

Be realistic about what you can and cannot do. Say, for example, "I certainly can't lift 125 pounds anymore, but I can lift more 50 pound weights in one day that when I was younger. That's because I've learned how to pace myself."

"I've learned to channel my energies so that I don't waste as much as I used to."

"I manage my time better and in the process I've increased my stamina."

DON'T TRY TO HIDE A PROBLEM WHICH MIGHT AFFECT YOUR PERFORMANCE, IF THE MATTER COMES UP. Your attitude means much more than any disability which can be compensated for. Be open and positive about it. Say, for example,

"Although I've had this condition for the past year, I've learned to compensate for it by strengthening my other abilities,"

"I can't use my right hand as well as I used to, but I've learned to write with my left hand and now I can do better with it than I could with my right hand."

"I've learned to avoid accidents by not taking unreasonable risks. I'm more careful than I used to be when I was 25; consequently, I have fewer accidents now and I make fewer mistakes."

 Technology is the knack of so arranging the world that we don't have to experience it. —Max Frisch

IF YOU DWELL ON THE P...
THE PRESENT AND FUTURE,
Y O U R S E L F . Discuss
plans to take adult education
courses, talk about your career
ambitions within the company,
inform them of your interest in
the latest technologies. Be forward looking.

IF YOU'RE USED TO
SUPERVISING OTHERS,
AVOID APPEARING
BOSSY. Give exam-
ples which show you can be a
good teamworker and can take
orders from persons in authority
who are younger than you are.

SMILE AT THE RECEPTIONIST AND SEC-
RETARY. It's not only polite, it's in your
best interest. The interviewer may later ask them,
"Well, what was your impression of .....?"

THE EVENING BEFORE THE INTERVIEW

𝒜 SSEMBLE THE INFORMATION YOU'LL NEED:
   * Social Security number, union or association
membership card, driver's license, etc.
   * Persons you will use as references: names, addresses and phone numbers.
   * Former employers and supervisors: names, addresses
and phone numbers.
   * Job titles you've held, dates of employment, your
major responsibilities and accomplishments. (Bring your
resume to jog your memory.)
   * Volunteer work experience: names, addresses,
phone numbers; dates you started and left; major responsibilities.
   * Education and Training: schools and colleges attended; dates of graduation or completion of courses;
certificates, diplomas, degrees or education units earn-

...nd honors ...t to your spe-...npetence for the

* Extra-curricular and leisure activities: hobbies and interests; sports activities (especially team sports); leadership positions held; special projects or anything else which highlights your job relevant interests, abilities and experience. Generally, a job application form doesn't have much space in which to list your achievements at length, so include only the most relevant, recent and impressive ones.

* Transportation: Learn the best route to get there. Find out how long it takes, and leave at least 45 minutes earlier in case of delays and to give yourself time to relax and get used to the surroundings.

ASSEMBLE THE THINGS YOU'LL NEED:
* Evidence of your abilities and achievements that can tip the scale in your favor (e.g., photocopies of commendations and awards; photographs; art or design work; published writings; graphs and charts which illustrate your productivity).

If you have slides or a videotape which make a point phone ahead so arrangements can be made to show them.

* Company items which demonstrate your eagerness to be part of the team and that you've done your homework (e.g., annual report, logos, samples, brochures, advertisements).

* "Tools" you'll need: pens or pencils; several copies of your resume; a pocket stapler to attach your resume to the job application form; a small notebook in which to write information you might forget such as interviewer's name, tax deductible job hunting expenses, and ways to improve your next interview.

* Set the breakfast table. Have the coffee or tea pot ready so you'll save time in the morning.

* Lay out the clothing you'll wear. Check for rips, runs and spots. Make sure they fit. Wear shoes that

don't pinch so you'll be comfortable during the interview.

* Transportation: If you're driving, check to see that the car runs and has plenty of gas. Have sufficient coins ready for parking meters and toll collectors. If you are taking public transportation, have plenty of coins or tokens ready.

SEVERAL NIGHTS BEFORE THE INTERVIEW, GO TO BED EARLIER THAN USUAL so you'll be refreshed and rested when the moment of truth arrives. If you wait to do this the night before the interview, you're likely to toss and turn and wake up feeling rotten.

Avoid caffeine (e.g., coffee, tea and chocolate). A low protein, high carbohydrate bedtime snack like milk with cereal, toast or a danish will help you sleep more soundly.

THE MORNING OF THE INTERVIEW

GET UP AT LEAST ONE HOUR EARLIER SO YOU'LL HAVE TIME TO DRESS WITHOUT HASTE AND LEAVE EARLY.

A HIGH PROTEIN, LOW CARBOHYDRATE BREAKFAST WILL WAKE YOU UP AND MAKE YOU MORE ALERT. Make sure it's light; a heavy meal will make you feel sluggish.

REVIEW your qualifications for the job, the questions you plan to ask and key points of yours response to the questions you may be asked.

TAKE A BRISK WALK JUST BEFORE THE INTERVIEW. You'll arrive smiling, relaxed and with good

179

color on your cheeks. If the weather is bad, do some tension relieving exercises in the company lounge. Take a few deep breaths, stretch your muscles, raise and lower your shoulders, touch your toes, or put your head down between your knees.

ARRIVE ABOUT 10 MINUTES EARLIER THAN SCHEDULED so you'll have time to get used to the surroundings. Arriving too early may give you time to worry and get nervous. Go to the company lounge and check your clothes, hair and makeup.

AFTER THE INTERVIEW

THANK THE INTERVIEWER BEFORE LEAVING, AND IF YOU ARE STILL INTERESTED IN THE JOB, SAY SO. Add that you are confident you can do it well. Since most job applicants neglect to say this, it will give you a competitive edge. If you don't express your interest, the interviewer will assume you are lukewarm about the job.

EVEN IF THE JOB LOOKS LIKE A SURE BET, DON'T CANCEL OTHER INTERVIEWS YOU HAVE LINED UP; KEEP LOOKING. It does happen that funds for a job opening are suddenly withdrawn or the job category itself is cancelled as an economizing measure.

This happened to a man who received a written job offer as department head in a state agency. He put his house up for sale and made other arrangements to move. Then the telegram bearing the bad news that funds had been cancelled arrived. Fortunately, he had a good lawyer and the job offer was restituted.

WRITE A BRIEF THANK YOU LETTER which restates your interest in working for the company. Summarize key points covered during the interview and include any which were omitted. Try to get this all on one page. Some experts advise attaching a one page post-interview resume which highlights your special qualifications for the job.

Many interviewers say this can be the deciding factor

since very few job applicants show this courtesy.
Send the letter the very same day or the day after
the interview.

ABOUT A WEEK LATER, FOLLOW UP THE LETTER
WITH A PHONE CALL to ask if it was
received. This, too, shows keen interest.

DON'T BE DISCOURAGED IF YOU GET RE-
JECTIONS, EVEN LOTS OF THEM. It happens to
everyone, even to highly skilled, well educated persons.
As one 32 year old college graduate put it, "The more
rejections I get, the harder it is. I have to keep
reminding myself that as one door closes, another will
open."

Persistence generally pays off, as long as you don't
make a pest of yourself. There's the case of a woman who
wanted a copywriter job, even though she had not completed college and had little experience in that field.
But the results of aptitude tests indicated high potential in the occupation. It took about nine phone calls
in as many months before she was finally hired. (A job
opening had not been advertised. She simply selected the
employer she wanted to work for.) Two things about her
he was sure of were her talent and her eagerness to work
for that particular company.

A college graduate applied, and was rejected three
times, for a management trainee job at Macy's in New
York City. On the fourth try, he decided to substitute a
one page, well written, informational letter for his
resume. He got the job.

MONEY magazine reports another form of persistence. A
recent college graduate had her heart set on being a
television news reporter. Knowing she faced formidable
competition, she took a low paying job as receptionist
in a local TV station. Then, she spent hours after work
doing odd jobs on a voluntary basis. This gave her an
opportunity to acquire good will with the employer and
lots of valuable experience which eventually helped her
land the dream job.

  *When you want something, go back and go back, and don't take "No!" for
an answer. And when rejection comes, don't take it personally. It goes
with the territory. Expose yourself to as much humiliation as you can bear,
then go home and do it all again tomorrow.*

— Betty Furness

EVERY MONTH OR SO, CONTACT EMPLOYERS WHO EXPRESSED INTEREST BUT WERE UNABLE TO HIRE YOU. Very often, they can only select one from among several equally well qualified applicants. A brief letter saying you would like to be considered when another opening occurs is a sincere form of flattery. Who knows? The person hired may not work out. Furthermore, employers have been known to send a rejection notice as a way of testing the applicant's assertiveness and interest.

TIMING IS CRUCIAL. As soon as you learn about a job opening, mail your resume without delay. Don't forget to follow up several days later with a phone call to ask if it was received.

IF YOU DON'T HEAR FROM THE EM-PLOYER AFTER A REASONABLE LENGTH OF TIME, OR IF YOU RECEIVE A REJECTION NOTICE, send a second resume or letter. It does happen that a resume is lost in the flood of applications. Others are rejected after careless reading. The same resume or letter may be read by two different screeners and get contradictory responses. The same screener will accept a resume on a day he/she is feeling good and reject it on a bad day.

A college professor who was changing careers applied for a job with a publishing firm. A few days after receiving a rejection, she resubmitted the same resume and cover letter. This time she was asked to come in for an interview.

A business executive applied directly to a company and was turned down. He then registered with two recruiting firms. Each submitted his qualifications to the very same employer, with no results. Finally, he answered a blind newspaper ad and was invited to an interview. It turned out to be the same company!

DON'T GIVE IN TO DEPRESSION AND A FEEL-ING OF HOPELESSNESS. Job hunting is like skiing. There are lots of ups and downs, lots of excitement, and the more you do it, the better you get.

There are far more questions here than you'll be asked in a 10 to 20 minute interview. Additional questions have been used in previous chapters to illustrate key points. Obviously, not every question is appropriate to your situation.

There are two basic types of questions--the factual and the probing or psychological. Each is designed to elicit different kinds of information from you.

Know exactly what is being asked before replying. If you're not sure ask, "As I understand your question, you want to know ...... Is that correct?"

For certain job openings (those involving much public contact, deadlines and/or competition) the interviewer may deliberately try to unnerve you, challenge you, or raise your self-doubts. He/She may purposely ask an embarrassing or provoking question or keep you waiting a long time in order to test your poise and ability to handle frustration. Blow your top or lose your cool and your out.

This is known as the stress interview. The purpose is to:

* See how logical you can be when your heart is in your mouth and your pulse is racing.
* See how cool you are when under pressure.
* See whether you have enough self-confidence to counteract people's doubts about your overall competence or specific qualifications for the job. This trait is especially important for jobs requiring persuading and influencing people (e.g., sales, training, public relations).
* Assess your creativity and flexibility from your spontaneous, unrehearsed answers to unexpected questions.

Tactics used in a stress interview vary. The interviewer may:

* Ask a provoking or even an offensive question ("Why should we hire you? Your resume gives no indication that you're better than the run-of-the mill applicant for this job," or "The last person who had this job didn't work out. Your qualifications seem to be no better. What makes you think you're superior?")
* Bluntly disagree with you or deliberately challenge you.
* Demonstrate disinterest, disdain or displeasure. (The interviewer avoids eye contact, or stares coldly at you, or fails to respond when you expect him/her to say something.)
* Keep you waiting an interminably long time.

The key element in a stress interview is surprise--using the unexpected to put you off balance. Knowing in advance that this might occur prepares you to face it. Think of it as a game in which your wits are pitted against the interviewer's. Pretend you are a salesperson on a challenging, fun assignment (e.g. selling an air conditioner to an Eskimo).

Do not take personally what appears to be hostility or dislike directed against you.

Keep in mind that there are no right or wrong answers to most of the interviewer's questions. What counts is the manner in which you respond.

FACTUAL QUESTIONS

* "If we hire you, how long do you expect to stay with us?"
* "Why did you quit your last job?"
* "How did you get along with your previous employer?"
* "How did you get along with your co-workers?"
* "Why have you had so many jobs?"
* "How would your previous employer describe you?"
* "How would your coworkers describe you?"
* "Why do you want to work for us?" (*A personnel recruiter put it this way, "People who say they want to work for us because it's such a great company score a lot of points, let's face it.*")
* "Where do you want to be five years from now?"
* "What are your long range goals?"
* "What do you expect to achieve at our company that you cannot elsewhere?"
* "What about this job interests you the most? (the least?)"
* "Why do you want to change careers after so many years?"
* "What did you like most (least) about your last job?"
* "What type of work are you interested in?" (*Keep the door open for other, related positions in the organization for which you are now, or will be, qualified. After describing your qualifications for this opening, say something to this effect, "I'm willing to consider other openings where my abilities and experience will be utilized.*")
* "Why have you chosen (----) as a career?"
* "Why should we hire you and not someone else with the same qualifications?"

185

* "What, in your opinion, are the qualities that make for a good (accountant)?"

* "What are some of the strengths you bring to this job?"

* "What are your weaknesses?" *(If you say something like this, "I really can't think of any," you won't make the great impression you expect. The interviewer might think you are conceited, insincere or plain dumb. An applicant who admits to some weaknesses is seen as being more honest. Slant your description of your "weak" points in such a way that you come out smelling like a rose.)*

* "What have you learned in your previous jobs that will help you in this one?"

* "Which position in our organization would you choose if you had the opportunity?" *(Don't fence yourself into one job. Apply what you've learned about job families to describe how your abilities fit into a variety of job niches. This is also a good opportunity to display your knowledge about the company.)*

* "What type of work would you do if you had the choice?"

* "Do you prefer routine work that is clearly defined or work that requires originality and problem solving?"

* "How good are you when working under pressure?" *(Back up your statements with examples.)*

* "What were the biggest problems you had to face in your previous job and how did you resolve them?"

* "What were some of the biggest mistakes you made in your previous job?" *(Show that you have learned from the experience.)*

* "What kind of supervisor do you prefer?" *(The interviewer wants to know if you are a teamworker who doesn't have to be continually told what to do.)*

* "Are you good at supervising others?" *(Give examples.)*

* "How would you feel working for a younger boss and with much younger coworkers?" *(Give examples of how well you get along with younger coworkers, especially those in a supervisory position.)*

* "Are you willing to work overtime?"

* "Are you willing to relocate if we open a branch

in (Haines, Alaska)?"

* "Which of your work experiences are professional and which are voluntary?" (*Say "All my work is professional" and go on to describe those abilities involved in your non-paid work which are transferable to the present job.*)

* "At what level in our organization do you see yourself?"

* "What were your most important accomplishments in your previous jobs?"

* "Are you considering other positions at this time?"

* "Why have you stayed with ---- employer for so long?" (*The interviewer is probably concerned about your ability to adjust to change.*)

* "How did you get your previous job?"

* "Is there anything in your personal life which will interfere with your ability to get the work done?"

* "How many days did you miss from work in your last job? Can you tell me the reason?" (*If you are a woman, the interviewer may be trying to find out if you have child care problems. Since it's illegal to ask about it directly, this is an indirect way to extract the information from you.*)

* "Aren't you overqualified for this job?" (*This may be a sneaky way of asking "Aren't you too old for the job?" The interviewer wants assurance that your energy level matches the demands of the job, that your experience and qualifications as a mature employee will be assets to the firm.*

Or, if you are making a radical career change, such

as from teaching to a business career, the interviewer
may wonder if you'll quit at
the earliest opportunity. You
can allay such doubts by:

Describing how the abilities required in your profession are transferable to the present job. Draw as
many parallels as possible between the two.

Assuring the interviewer that you have no intention
of going back to the old career by pointing out its
negative aspects (e.g., low salary, poor advancement
opportunities).

Avoiding the use of fancy vocabulary and jargon from
your old profession. Use the buzzwords of the new one in
order to show that you have made a clean break.

Don't expect your M.A. or Ph.D. to get you the job.
Some employers view it as a liability. Others might be
intimidated by it.

PROBING QUESTIONS are designed to
elicit information about your personality and interests; your attitudes toward work, authority, political
and social issues; and your energy level. The interviewer cannot ask you point blank, "Do you go to pieces when
under pressure?" One way to get such information is
through probing questions.

For example, the former head of a Federal agency used
as a point of discussion in job interviews. If an applicant were a Pisces, she would mention the tendency of
this group to go in two different directions, and ask if
the applicant also has this problem. Then she would
causally mention that Ralph Nader is a Pisces and watch
to see if the applicant appears indignant or flattered.
(Nader is a well known liberal consumer activist.)

Although it's important to convey sincerity, it is
not dishonest to slant your answers so as to emphasize
your best qualities. Anything you say which reassures
the interviewer that you are the right person for the
job will be appreciated.

* "Do you feel you need any room for improvement?"
* "What have you learned from your past mistakes?"
(The interviewer wants to know if you are still growing

as a person, how well you deal with your mistakes.)

* "In what way has college prepared you for the real world?"

* "How did you like college?"

* "Do you think it's a good school? Explain why" (or, why not).

* "Tell me about an experience you had before the age of 20 which gave you the greatest sense of fulfillment." *(The interviewer wants to know if your basic personality and interests match the job and the company. These and similar questions are the basic ingredients of interest inventories which are administered by career counselors.)*

* "What is the most difficult situation you ever experienced and how did you resolve it?"

* "What is the most wonderful situation you ever experienced?"

* "Tell me about a time you did something that you are especially proud of. Why are you proud?"

* "What do you do in your spare time?"

* "Tell me about yourself." *(Mention only those aspects which demonstrate your suitability for the job: hobbies which utilize the same abilities and interests; personality traits that fit the job; volunteer work and membership in organizations where you exercised some of the abilities required by the job.)*

CAUTION: This is an open-ended question which can lure you into telling your life story and other irrelevancies. That's not the purpose of the question. The interviewer may also want to see how focused your thoughts are. Be concise. Get to the point.

Or, the interviewer may present a problem and then ask what you would do in the situation. Here are some examples:

"You are working on a team project and one of your coworkers is very difficult." (He/She argues over trivialities, comes in late from lunch, takes credit for your work, spreads false rumors, etc.)

"A worker in your office has gotten into the habit of taking 10 to 15 minutes longer for lunch, and this forces you to take over her phone calls and other responsibilities which can't be put off."

"A new department head who has just been promoted to the job gives you a verbal go-ahead to spend upwards of $40,000 for computer equipment and other improvements in the department. Several weeks after you make the purchases, the chief executive officer comes raging in. You learn the department head lacked the authority to okay the expense. He denies knowing anything about it, and you are left holding the bag."

QUESTIONS THE INTERVIEWER SHOULD NOT ASK

UNDER FEDERAL LAW, IT'S ILLEGAL FOR EMPLOYERS TO ASK QUESTIONS ABOUT RACE, AGE, NATIONAL ORIGIN, SEX AND RELIGION. These classes of people are protected: racial minorities, women, religious minorities, people over 40, and people of certain national origins.

There are other laws which protect the handicapped and ex-offenders (including rehabilitated drug and alcohol abusers) from discrimination in employment.

The only exception is when the occupation or business justifies refusing to hire someone in the protected categories. For example, Dolly Parton could justifiably be refused a role portraying General Custer.

However, a woman or a Black who is refused a sales job on the grounds that the company's customers prefer dealing with white males has sufficient grounds for claiming discrimination.

HOWEVER, IT IS LEGAL FOR AN EMPLOYER TO ASK SUCH QUESTIONS AFTER YOU ARE HIRED. The employer can, for example, ask for proof of age or about your medical history for insurance purposes.

THE LAW REQUIRES EMPLOYERS TO CONSIDER ONLY JOB RELATED FACTORS AND YOUR PRESENT ABILITY TO DO THE WORK. If, for example, the employer requires a high school diploma for a messenger job, it may be an attempt to discriminate against members of minority groups who have

190

a high dropout rate. Or, if the employer gives a woman a test to see if she can lift 100-pound weights for a job which involves lifting no more than 25-pound weights, it may be an illegal means to eliminate female candidates.

IN SOME STATES IT IS ILLEGAL TO ASK QUESTIONS ABOUT THE FOLLOWING MATTERS:

✳ A request to see your birth certificate, driver's license, or any other indicator of age.

✳ Height and weight. (In 1985, a woman won a lawsuit against a corporation on the grounds that she was wrongfully refused a job as systems analyst because she was grossly overweight. The judge ruled her weight was irrelevant to her ability to do the work required.)

✳ Past illnesses or a physical disability which does not interfere with your ability to do the work.

✳ Arrests not followed by a conviction. It is legal, however, to ask about criminal convictions or to refuse to hire a convicted felon on the grounds that the employer will be unable to bond the person. (In some cases it is illegal to ask about convictions which occurred as a youthful offender.)

✳ Whether you ever had psychiatric treatment, taken addictive drugs or had a problem with alcohol. (However, in 1985 IBM and several other large corporations began requiring applicants for jobs at all levels to pass a urinalysis test for drugs and alcohol. This is a result of an "epidemic of cocaine casualties" in the U.S. workforce, according to the National Institute on Drug Abuse.)

✳ Marital status, plans to get married, and child care arrangements.

AN EMPLOYER WHO ASKS A WOMAN THE FOLLOWING QUESTIONS IS VIOLATING FEDERAL OR STATE LAWS WHICH PROHIBIT DISCRIMINATION AGAINST WOMEN.

✳ Are you engaged? Do you plan to get married?

✳ Do you plan to have children?

✳ Who takes care of your children?

✳ How does your husband feel about your traveling on business?

Neither flatter wealth nor cringe before power. —Anonymous

YOU DO NOT HAVE TO ANSWER ILLEGAL QUESTIONS. But, be careful not to reply bluntly: "That's none of your business" or "I won't tell you because it's illegal for you to ask such a question."

Be tactful: "I think my experience and qualifications are excellent for the job and I don't see why my [age] has anything to do with it," or "Is that necessary for the job?"

If the interviewer starts probing into your personal life say something tactful (e.g., "I'd like to be as helpful as possible, but I don't see what my personal life has to do with the requirements of the job.") Better yet, assure the interviewer there is nothing in your personal life which will interfere with your ability to do the work.

QUESTIONS YOU MAY WANT TO ASK

Ask questions at appropriate times or when the interviewer seems to be finished and you will make a better impression. Be careful not to appear to take over the interview, however.

* "What are the regular duties of the job?"
* "When things get busy, what else will the person hired be expected to do?"
* "What is a typical day on the job like?"
* "How much overtime work is there? Is it seasonal or on a continuing basis?" (If continuing: "How many hours a week/month on the average?")
* "What kind of person do you want for this job?"
* "What are some of the biggest problems to be resolved in this job?"
* "Where does the job lead?"
* "How can the person hired attain that goal?"
* "Does the company prefer to promote from within or from the outside?"
* "Are there any barriers to moving from one division or department to another?" (Ask this only of a personnel specialist, not a department head.)
* "What does the company do to help its employees advance?"
* "Does the company have training programs?" "Which

employees are eligible?" "Will you describe the programs?"

* "Does the company provide for tuition reimbursement for continuing education?" "For what type of courses?" "What are the maximum number of credits allowed?" "How much of the tuition is paid for?" "Is every employee entitled to this?"

* "What is the turnover rate in the company?" "In this department?"

* "Is this vacancy the result of a company expansion, a promotion or did someone leave?" (If it was due to a promotion, ask why the previous employee was promoted so you'll have an idea of the company's standards. Ask what position the person holds now.)

* "Why did the person who last held this job leave?" (If the person was fired, ask why so that you'll know what to avoid.)

* "How is job performance evaluated?" "How often?" "Who will do the evaluating?" (This information will help you to assess your own performance.)

* "How often will there be a salary review?"

* "Which aspects of the job do you consider to be most important?"

* "To whom does the person hired for this job report?"

* "May I meet that person?" (Ask this only if a job offer seems forthcoming.)

* "Which positions would be among the first to be eliminated if there should be a company wide retrenchment?"

* "Can you tell me something about the financial stability of this company?" (Ask this if it's a small, new business. Try to get information on debts, earnings, rate of growth, whether the growth is due to increased sales or to a merger or acquisition, percentage of long term debt to total capital, etc.)

* "What management style does the company prefer?"

* "What are the people in the department like?"

* "May I talk to someone in the department?" (Try to get information on the least attractive aspects of the work and the company, opportunities that are available and what to avoid.)

* "May I see where the person hired will be work-

193

ing?" (Also watch for the following clues: dress code, general maintenance, general attitude of the employees, work piled high on desks, whether relations with supervisors seem strained or relaxed.)

* "Are there any other advantages to this job?"

* "How much flexibility do your employees have regarding (hours of work, clothing to wear, vacation schedules, lunch time, etc.)?"

* "Are there any disadvantages?"

* "What sort of job security do you offer new employees?"

* "What medical insurance plan does the company provide?" "Can you tell me what specifically is covered?" (If the company does not pay 100% of hospitalization costs, ask why.)

* "What kind of pension (or profit sharing) plan does the company have?"

* "When can I expect to hear the results of the interview?"

SOME PUBLISHED INFORMATION SOURCES

1. "Impressions of personality in the employment interview," by Douglas N. Jackson, et. al., JOURNAL OF PERSONALITY AND SOCIAL PSYCHOLOGY, 1980, vol 39(2).

2. "Understanding and assessing nonverbal expressiveness," by Howard S. Friedman, et. al., JOURNAL OF PERSONALITY AND SOCIAL PSYCHOLOGY, 1980, VOL 39(2).

3. "Male and female spoken language differences: Stereotypes and evidence," by Adelaide Haas, JOURNAL OF PERSONALITY AND SOCIAL PSYCHOLOGY, 1979, vol. 56(3).

4. BODY LANGUAGE by J. Fast (Pocketbooks, 1971).

5. "Workplace high-tech spurs retraining efforts," by Dwight B. Davis, HIGH TECHNOLOGY, November 1984.

6. "Nonverbal communication: Implications for and use by counselors," Stella L. Norman, 1982, INDIVIDUAL PSYCHOLOGY, vol. 38(4).

7. "Action therapy," by W. E. O'Connell, 1978, INDIVIDUAL PSYCHOLOGY, Vol.15.

8. KINESICS AND CONTEXT by R.L. Birdwhistle (University of Pennsylvania Press, 1970).

9. "High-tech superachievers float their way to success," by Tom Shea, INFOWORLD, January 23, 1984.

10. "Effects of previewing the application on interview process and outcomes," by Robert L. Dipboye, et. al., JOURNAL OF APPLIED PSYCHOLOGY, 1984, vol. 69(1).

11. "Effect of interview length and applicant quality on interview decision," by William Tullar, et. al., JOURNAL OF APPLIED PSYCHOLOGY, 1980, vol. 65(4) 1979, vol. 64(6);

12. "Impressions of personality in the employment interview," by Douglas N. Jackson, et. al., JOURNAL OF APPLIED PSYCHOLOGY, 1980, vol. 65(2).

13. "An empirical construct validity approach to studying predictor-job performance links," by Walter C. Borman, et. al., JOURNAL OF APPLIED PSYCHOLOGY, 1980, vol.65(6).

14. "The situational interview," by Gary P. Latham, et. al., JOURNAL OF APPLIED PSYCHOLOGY, 1980, vol.65(4).

15. "Factor analysis of Strong Vocational Interest Blank Items," by James Rounds, Jr. & Rene Dawes, JOURNAL OF APPLIED PSYCHOLOGY, 1979, vol. 64(2).

16. "Another look at contrast effects in the employment interview," by Frank Landy & Frederick Bates, JOURNAL OF APPLIED PSYCHOLOGY, 1974, vol 58(1).

17. "Individual differences in the decision process of employment interviewers," by Enzo Valenzi & I. R. Andrews, JOURNAL OF APPLIED PSYCHOLOGY, 1973, vol. 58(1).

18. "Estimating the influence of job information on interviewer agreement," by John Langdale, JOURNAL OF APPLIED PSYCHOLOGY, 1973, vol. 57(1).

19. "Training interviewers to eliminate contrast effects in employment interviews," by Kenneth Wexley, et. al., JOURNAL OF APPLIED PSYCHOLOGY, 1973, vol 57(3).

20. "Response requirements and primacy-recency effects in a simulated selection interview," by James L. Farr, JOURNAL OF APPLIED PSYCHOLOGY, 1973, vol. 57(3).

21. "Interview decisions as determined by competency and attitude similarity," by Glenn Baskett, JOURNAL OF APPLIED PSYCHOLOGY, 1973, vol. 57(3).

22. "Fat, four-eyed and female," by Mary B. Harris, et. al. JOURNAL OF APPLIED SOCIAL PSYCHOLOGY, 1982 vol. 12(6).

23. "Weapons and eye contact as instigators or inhibitors of aggressive arousal in police-citizen interaction," by Ehor O. Boyanowsky & Curt T. Griffiths, JOURNAL OF APPLIED SOCIAL PSYCHOLOGY, 1982, vol. 12(5).

24. "Effects of self-administered cognitive therapy on social evaluation anxiety," by Stewart Schelver & Kenneth Gutsch, JOURNAL OF CLINICAL PSYCHOLOGY, 1983, vol. 39(5).

25. "Prosocial behavior as affected by eye contact, touch and voice expression," Morton Goldman & Jerry Fordyce, JOURNAL OF SOCIAL PSYCHOLOGY, 1983, vol. 121.

26. "Halo effect of an initial impression upon speaker and audience," by Morton Goldman, et. al., JOURNAL OF SOCIAL PSYCHOLOGY 1983, Vol. 120.

27. "Who's There? Interviewing Techniques For Small Businesses," NATIONAL CHILD LABOR COMMITTEE, 1501 Broadway, New York, NY 10036.

28. "Job loyalty: Not the virtue it seems," by Jeanne McDowell, THE NEW YORK TIMES, March 3, 1985.

29. "What's new in employment testing," by David Tuller, THE NEW YORK TIMES, February 24, 1985.

30. "Putting the disabled to work: Major effort at DuPont," by N.R Kleinfield, THE NEW YORK TIMES, April 12, 1984.

31. "Social anxiety: New focus leads to insights and therapy," by Daniel Goleman, THE NEW YORK TIMES, December 18, 1984.

32. "Some sad people, it seems, are unhappy as a matter of habit," by Tom Ferrell, THE NEW YORK TIMES, November 15, 1983.

33. "Improving personnel selection," by Calvin Hoffman, et. al., PACE/Piedmont Airlines, September 1984.

34. "Influence of information about ability and non-ability in personnel selection decisions," by William Griffett & Thomas Jackson, PSYCHOLOGICAL REPORTS, 1970, vol. 20.

35. THE SILENT LANGUAGE by Edward Hall (Greenwood, 1980).

36. "Women clash: Older worker vs. young boss," THE WALL STREET JOURNAL, February 19, 1985.

37. "Smokestack managers moving to high-tech find the going tough," by John Bussey, THE WALL STREET JOURNAL, January 10, 1985.

38. "Women executives feel that men both aid and hinder their careers," by Helen Rogan, THE WALL STREET JOURNAL, October 29, 1984.

39. "Top women executives find path to power is strewn with hurdles," by Helen Rogan, THE WALL STREET JOURNAL, October 25, 1984

40. "Single parents who raise children feel stretched thin by home, job," by Betsy Morris, THE WALL STREET JOURNAL, September 28, 1984.

41. "Dose of smiles is latest prescription for hospitals that vie for patients," by David Mills, THE WALL STREET JOURNAL, September 24, 1984.

42. "Rules that apply after a worker has clocked out," by Larry Stessin, THE WALL STREET JOURNAL, September 24, 1984.

43. "ITT chief emphasizes harmony, confidence & playing by rules," by Monica Langley, THE WALL STREET JOURNAL, September 13, 1984.

44. "Companies sponsor diet programs to help workers shed pounds, raise productivity," by Carmen J. Lee, THE WALL STREET JOUR58 NAL, August 9, 1984.

45. "Women in electronics find Silicon Valley best and worst," THE WALL STREET JOURNAL, March 2, 1984.

APPENDIX

OCCUPATIONS AND THE JOB MARKET

THE AMERICAN ALMANAC OF JOBS AND SALARIES by John B. Wright (Avon Books, 1984). Gives job descriptions, salary ranges, advancement opportunities, and tells where the best job prospects for each occupation are.

900,000 PLUS JOBS ANNUALLY: PUBLISHED SOURCES OF EMPLOYMENT LISTINGS, by S. Norman Feingold and Glenda A. Hansard-Winkler (Garret Park Press, 1982).

Write to CATALYST (250 Park Avenue South, New York, N.Y. 10003; phone number 212-777-8900) for inexpensive pamphlets on a wide range of occupations, from accounting to urban planning. Ask for a free list.

ENCYCLOPEDIA OF CAREERS AND VOCATIONAL GUIDANCE (in 3 volumes); editor, William Hopke (Doubleday, 1984). Information on job responsibilities, education and other requirements, job outlook and salary for over 350 occupations.

EMPLOYMENT OPPORTUNITIES FOR THE HANDICAPPED (World Trade Academy Press, N.Y.). After each occupational description, gives the types of handicaps which would not interfere with job performance.

PETERSON'S GUIDE TO ENGINEERING, SCIENCE AND COMPUTER JOBS (Peterson's Guides)

The following are published by the Bureau of Labor Statistics, U.S. Department of Labor. You can order a copy from the Superintendent of Documents, U.S. Government Printing Office, Washington, D.C. 20402. You can also buy the books at a local U.S. Government bookstore. Most libraries have reference copies.

THE DIRECTORY OF OCCUPATIONAL TITLES gives descriptions for over 34,000 occupations. Although it does not have information on prospects, salaries, requirements and employers, it does give a detailed picture of what the job entails

OCCUPATIONAL OUTLOOK FOR COLLEGE GRADUATES lists occupations (and related occupations) for which a college degree is desired. Lists professional associations which offer more detailed information on specialized fields within each profession, future employment prospects and salary ranges.

OCCUPATIONAL OUTLOOK HANDBOOK, 1986-87 edition. Gives detailed information on over 250 occupations. Also lists professional societies, trade associations, labor unions, government agencies, private companies and educational institutions which offer more detailed information on a specific occupation. The Handbook is updated every two years.
Describes many aspects of each occupation (i.e., earnings, job prospects, working conditions, related occupations, what the work is like, personality requirements, opportunities for advancement, training and education requirements, and where to find additional information.)
Reprints on job families (clusters of related occupations) from the Handbook can be purchased singly. Useful to the job hunter who wants to learn about a specific occupation or job family. Send for a free list by writing to your regional office of the Bureau of Labor Statistics or the nearest U.S. Government Bookstore.

OCCUPATIONAL OUTLOOK QUARTERLY describes new occupations, their training opportunities, salary ranges, and long term job prospects. Also gives information on how to choose an occupation and find a job.

SALARIES, BENEFITS AND PERKS

SALARY STRATEGIES: EVERYTHING YOU NEED TO KNOW TO GET THE SALARY YOU WANT, by Marilyn Moats Kennedy (Rawson Associates, 1982).

EMPLOYERS AND INDUSTRIES

SUPER-DIRECTORIES include employer directories for various industries and directories on associations and publications in every field. If you don't know where to start looking, start with these.

* GUIDE TO AMERICAN DIRECTORIES (B. Klein Publications)

* DIRECTORY OF DIRECTORIES (Gale Research Company)

DIRECTORIES of business firms and trade and professional associations are an important information source for the serious job hunter. Private industry directories, for example, describe each company's major activities; number of employees; and give names, addresses, and phone numbers of persons to contact.

❋❋❋❋❋❋❋

THE AMERICAN BANK DIRECTORY

AMERICAN CORPORATE FAMILIES (Dun & Bradstreet) lists names and addresses of major corporations, parent companies and subsidiary businesses. Categorized by geographical area and products.

BUSINESS ORGANIZATIONS AND AGENCIES DIRECTORY (Gale Research Co.) is a guide to private and public organizations which provide information on business and industry.

BUSINESS PERIODICALS INDEX is where you'll find titles of newspaper, magazine and journal articles on business matters. Excellent source of up-to-the minute information on occupations, employers, industries, and the job market.

REFERENCE BOOK OF CORPORATE MANAGEMENTS (Dun and Bradstreet) lists over 31,000 businesses which have a net worth of between $500,00 and $1 million.

ENCYCLOPEDIA OF ASSOCIATIONS (Gale Research Co.) lists thousands of associations which can send you information on trade, business, professional, labor, scientific, educational, agriculture, social welfare, voluntary and social organizations, and other areas. Specific fields are also included, such as direct marketing, data processing and energy. Lists addresses and phone numbers, employment exchanges, reports and bulletins, newsletters and other services provided by the associations. Your public library probably has a copy.

ENCYCLOPEDIA OF BUSINESS INFORMATION SOURCES by Paul Wasserman (Gale Research Company, 1983).

FEDERAL GOVERNMENT (the U.S. Library of Congress) lists Federal information resources in the nation.

HOW TO FIND INFORMATION ABOUT COMPANIES: THE CORPORATE INTELLIGENCE SOURCE BOOK (Washington Researchers. Ltd., Washington, D.C. 20007).

IN SEARCH OF EXCELLENCE: LESSONS FROM AMERICA'S BEST-RUN COMPANIES by Thomas J. Peters and Robert H. Waterman, Jr. (Warner Books, 1985). On the best seller list.

LITERARY MARKETPLACE lists publishers, book manufacturers, editorial services, magazines, newspapers, public relations services, radio and TV stations. A must for writers, researchers, editors and word processors.

MILLION DOLLAR DIRECTORY lists 120,000 businesses with a net worth of $500,000 or more which are arranged alphabetically and geographically. Includes address, phone, annual sales, number of employees, division names and functions, and names, titles and functions of principal executives.

MOODY'S BANKS AND FINANCE MANUAL includes more than 10,000 national, state and private banks, insurance companies, mutual funds, mortgage and finance companies, real estate investment trusts, savings and loan and other financial institutions. Lists their headquarters and branch offices, names of directors and other top-level personnel, Moody's rating, and extensive financial and statistical data.

NATIONAL TRADE AND PROFESSIONAL ASSOCIATIONS OF THE UNITED STATES AND CANADA (Columbia Books) lists officers, addresses and phone numbers of over 5,000 labor unions; scientific and technical societies; business, trade and professional associations.

NATIONAL DIRECTORY OF ADDRESSES AND TELEPHONE NUMBERS (Bantam Books).

RAND-McNALLY INTERNATIONAL BANKER DIRECTORY lists over 15,000 banks and 37,000 branches, 500 of the largest commercial banks, as well as 40,000 foreign banks engaged in foreign trade. Includes: address, phone, principal officers and key financial data.

STANDARD & POOR'S REGISTER OF CORPORATIONS, DIRECTORS AND EXE-
CUTIVES lists over 45,000 corporations. Includes: address,
phone, products and services as well as names and titles of top
level directors and executives, their date and place of birth,
fraternal organization membership and other business affilia-
tions.

STANDARD RATE AND DATA lists all business periodicals.

THE 100 BEST COMPANIES TO WORK FOR IN AMERICA by Robert Lever-
ing, Milton Moskowitz and Michael Katz (Addison Wesley, 1984).
Describes pay, work environment, job security, employee benefits and perks, management-worker relations, policy regarding
layoffs and promotion from within the ranks, the value each
company places on its employees as compared with its capital
resources, and more. Also lists companies which have the best
training programs, practice little or no sex discrimination,
value graduate degrees, and those in which you can get ahead
without a college degree. A behind-the-scenes look which you
won't find in directories.

(Note: Make sure you get the current edition of books on employers and industries. Changes come so rapidly these days that
a company which is on the "best" list one year may easily
topple off the next year. Also, be aware that these books
generally describe only private industry employers and only the
most prominent. Nevertheless, if you are looking for a job in a
smaller company or a non-profit organization, you will find
these books a gold mine of criteria and standards to use.

THE (your state or region) JOB BANK (Bob Adams Inc., 2045
Commonwealth Avenue, Brighton, MA 02135). In 1984 there were
editions for Chicago; the Southwest; Texas; Pennsylvania; Washington, D.C.; Northern California; Southern California; Greater
Atlanta and Metropolitan New York. Editions on other cities and
areas are forthcoming.

Information on most major businesses in each area is given.
Basic activities of each company are summarized. Phone numbers,
addresses and names of persons to contact are included, as well
as salary ranges for each occupation. Typical career paths in
major occupations are also given. Includes additional lists

such as career counseling and employment services. This book does most of the slave labor for you.

THOMAS REGISTER OF AMERICAN MANUFACTURERS lists over 120,000 manufacturing firms in the U.S. arranged geographically, alphabetically and by produce and service. Includes names and titles of officers, number of employees, address and phone, capital assets, and parent and associate companies.

TRADE AND PROFESSIONAL ASSOCIATION DIRECTORY

THE WALL STREET INDEX lists all articles (categorized by names and topics) published in "The Wall Street Journal." A must, especially for finding out who's who and what's what on specific companies and industries.

WHO'S WHO IN COMMERCE AND INDUSTRY

NEWSPAPERS

Although only a small percentage of job openings are advertised in newspapers, many job hunters swear by them. Surveys show such ads rank well below personal contacts and direct contacts with employers as a source of jobs.

HOW HELPFUL ADS CAN BE DEPENDS ON THE TYPE OF JOB you're looking for. Ads for high-skill, executive, managerial and professional job openings are worth looking into. Ads for "Gal or Guy Friday" and other low-skill, low-paying jobs are more likely to result in disappointment. You'll do better by walking into a company's personnel office and filling out a job application form or by mailing in your resume with a snappy cover letter.

BLIND ADS which give only a box number (the employer's name and address are omitted) are said to be a waste of time. Some companies place them in order to get information on the labor market and salary levels or to test the loyalty of their employees.

OMNIBUS ADS which list a huge assortment of job openings at pay that seems too good to be true are often used as lures to get your name added to the employment agencies' list of clients.

ADS THAT SAY "NO EXPERIENCE NECESSARY" should be viewed with caution. The employer may be having difficulty filling the vacancy because of poor salary and/or working conditions.

CITY NEWSPAPERS which have a large circulation are more likely to have a special Sunday supplement which is devoted exclusively to help wanted ads. Although many of the job openings are local, quite a few are located in other cities and states.

OUT-OF-TOWN NEWSPAPERS are an excellent source of employers you can contact by mail or long distance phone call. You can follow up a phone inquiry with a resume or informational letter.

Some job hunters have succeeded in making an interview appointment by phone. When they arrive, they also make a tour of the community to get information on unadvertised job leads and a first-hand look at the living conditions. Other sections of these newspapers contain clues to the cost of living and quality of life in the community. Articles in the business section give clues to which industries and companies are thriving and, therefore, in a hiring mood.

A PROBLEM IN USING NEWSPAPER ADS is that you're competing with hundreds of other job hunters who have also seen the ad. Buy the newspaper as soon as it's issued. Stay up till midnight or get up at the crack of dawn, if necessary, and answer the ads without delay. Have a stack of resumes ready for such opportunities. Some job hunters send their resumes and cover letters by special delivery mail. Others send a second copy a day later just in case the first one gets buried beneath the pile.

LIBRARY SUBSCRIPTION COPIES OF OUT-OF-TOWN NEWSPAPERS generally arrive several days after they appear on the newsstands. Since every minute counts, find out when they usually arrive and get to the library as early as possible. Better yet, order a subscription if you can afford it. The librarian can give you information on subscriptions to the major city newspapers.

THE NATIONAL BUSINESS EMPLOYMENT WEEKLY lists job openings which are mostly at the executive, management and professional levels. Also has articles giving valuable advice on how to find the right job and advance in your career (i.e., "Better Cover Letters," "How To Survive With An Inferior Superior," "Resumes For Career Changers," "Finding a Job on Capitol Hill"). Single copies can be purchased at newsstands for $3.00. A 12-week subscription costs $47 and includes postage. Write to The Wall Street Journal, 420 Lexington Avenue, New York, NY 10170 or phone (212) 808-6792.

TRADE, UNION AND PROFESSIONAL ASSOCIATIONS

These associations also publish journals and newsletters which generally list job openings that newspapers don't carry as well as information on the latest events in the occupation and industry. The public library may have a file of association publications.

BUSINESS PERIODICALS
The library has periodical indexes of magazines which give up-to-date information on the national job market, industries and employers. These include "MONEY," "Time," "Forbes," "Business Week," "Newsweek," "Value Line Investment Survey," "Fortune," and others.

CHAMBER OF COMMERCE
If you are thinking of moving to another community, write to its Chamber of Commerce for information on housing costs and the job market. You might learn, before it's too late, that the community is actively discouraging job seekers from out of town.

HELP IN FINDING A JOB

NETWORKS AND PERSONAL CONTACTS

Networks are the modern equivalent of the "Old Boy" buddy system. They include organizations which have the specific purpose of helping persons who share certain characteristics find a job (age, sex, race, religion, ethnicity, occupation, and alumni associations).

They are also informal contacts such as the local banker, your lawyer, neighbors, friends, relatives, doctor, people you meet in job placement offices, ex-spouses, and anyone else who is in a position to help you locate a job opening or knows someone who can.

Most of the well-organized networks are for members of groups that are considered disadvantaged, such as women and racial, ethnic and religious minorities. The paucity of men's groups listed below is not due to the author's bias. There simply aren't as many self-help organizations listed for them. Men still have their old buddy systems.

Some of the self-help groups have job banks and job referral services for their members or clients.

Look in Gale's "Encyclopedia of Associations" for local equivalents or branches of the following organizations. Also look in your phone directory. The purpose of listing these few is to show you what's available out there to give you a helping hand.

CATALYST sponsors over 220 career information centers for women. Its services include a career resource library and, in some centers, test administration, career counseling and job placement. It also promotes the advancement of women in management and executive positions. It maintains dossiers of qualified women candidates which company chairmen have access to in order to find women to serve on their boards and for their top level positions. For a brochure listing women's networks which are affiliated with Catalyst, write to 250 Park Avenue South, New York, NY 10003 or phone 212-777-8900.

DISPLACED HOMEMAKER NETWORK, INC. helps women between the ages of 35 and 64 who have lost their means of support as a result of divorce or widowhood, who have minimal financial resources and are not eligible for unemployment insurance or Social Security benefits. There are nationwide programs which operate under the umbrella of Action, state departments of labor, and other government programs.

Its services include psychological counseling; social support; job referrals; referrals to adult education courses; on-the-job training; seminars and workshops on such topics as job readiness, how to be more assertive, how to deal effectively with your lawyer and money management.

Generally, there is no fee, although some centers may charge a fee based on ability to pay. For information on a program near you contact any of the following:

Displaced Homemaker, 1325 G Street, NW, Washington, D.C. 20005 (or phone 202/628-6767).

Your state's department of labor.

The local YWCA.

The Women's Bureau, U.S. Department of Labor, 200 Constitution Avenue, NW, Washington, D.C. 20210.

FORTY-PLUS is a nationwide, non-profit network of self-help groups for unemployed managers, executives and professionals who are forty years of age or older. To become a member you must be at least 40 years old, a U.S. citizen, unemployed and actively seeking a new job, and have held a recent executive, managerial or professional position. At least six references from former employers and business associates are also required. There is no discrimination based on color, race, religion or sex.

Since it is a self-sustaining cooperative, members are expected to help about 2-1/2 days per week in the business operations of the Club.

Members receive help in assessing their abilities, experience and personal characteristics in order to define their career goals. Expert coaching in resume preparation and techniques of job finding and interviewing is also available. Members may also use the Forty-Plus office as a base of operations, with telephone answering and mail service, typewriters, word processors, a reference library and a place to work and share information with one's peers.

Most members find jobs through their own efforts, and many find the job leads developed by the Club's Marketing Department invaluable. In 1984, members were able to find new positions with an average starting salary of $44,000. The average age of those who got jobs was over 52 and the length of stay at the Club ranged from three to seven months.

There is a membership fee of $300 plus a charge of $5.00 per week for "housekeeping" during active membership. When a member leaves to take a job, he or she pays an exit fee of $300. These funds are needed to pay the costs of operating the Club. Associate Membership entitles one to receive a periodic newsletter and information on new jobs available in their field.

The founding advisory board includes such notables as Thomas J. Watson, Jr., Chairman of the Board of IBM; Dr. Norman Vincent Peale of Marble Collegiate Church; and J. Peter Grace, Chairman of the Board of W.R. Grace & Company.

For the address of the nearest office, write to the Forty-Plus Club's main office at 15 Park Row, New York, N.Y. 10038 or phone 212-233-6086. If there is no club in your area, ask for information on how to start one.

 If you are willing to take the punishment, you are halfway through the battle.
—Lillian Hellman

NATIONAL NETWORK FOR WOMEN IN SALES has four regional offices which offer a placement service, a job bank, a resume file, advice on resume preparation, and career counseling. The headquarters are at P.O. Box 95269 (phone: 312/577-1944).

NATIONAL ORGANIZATION FOR WOMEN is a political action network to help women advance in the world of work. Career counseling and assertiveness training is offered in some chapters. The cost is based on ability to pay. There are 800 chapters nationwide. For the address of one near you write to the central office at 140 New York Avenue, NW, Suite 800, Washington, D.C. 20005-2102.

the U.S. DEPARTMENT OF LABOR, EMPLOYMENT AND TRAINING ADMINISTRATION, (601 D Street, NW, Washington, DC 20213) sponsors programs which include placement services and job training, including services for groups having special needs or difficulty entering or returning to the workforce. Among the programs are the following:

1. FEDERAL-STATE JOB SERVICE: Maintains local offices which offer job placement, career guidance and counseling, and referral and placement in apprenticeship programs. Under the Reagan administration, Federal support to states for this program has been slashed, and services in some communities have been drastically curtailed. Hopefully, the slack will be taken up by individual state departments of labor.

The services are free. The Job Service offices are said to have more job listings and more information on the local and national job markets than any other source. (Several states may not list their job vacancies with the diminishing Federal Service either because they lack funds or because they don't want to attract hordes of out-of-town job seekers.)

Be sure to get to the local Job Service office as soon as the doors open, and go regularly, because most of the job openings are filled almost as soon as they are listed. In order to get the best service possible, be prepared to tell the counselor exactly what you want. Bring all the information you would normally take to a job interview.

Some offices also provide career counseling which includes the administration and interpretation of tests to assess aptitudes and interests. You must ask for this; don't expect it to be offered to you.

In some states, special services are offered to certain categories of job seekers such as persons who have lost their jobs to high technology, women, persons over 45, displaced homemakers, veterans and the handicapped. Workers who have lost their jobs because of imports also qualify under the Trade Readjustment Allowance Act. Unemployed executives and professionals are also considered to be in need of special help because finding an appropriate job is more difficult for them than for white and blue collar workers.

Look in the phone book under your state's department of labor for division titles such as the following: Employment Service, Job Service Division, Division for Women, Office For The Aging, Vocational Rehabilitation, Job Training Programs, Apprenticeship and Training, Civil Service Department.

2. JOB TRAINING PARTNERSHIP PROGRAMS are sponsored and operated by a consortium of federal, state and private industry agencies and representatives. They function to train eligible persons in permanent, unsubsidized jobs, preferably in the private sector.

Classroom instruction in occupational skills, on-the-job training, career counseling, psychological testing and job placement are provided. Special help is given to the economically disadvantaged and persons who have lost or are about to lose their jobs to high-technology. Some assistance is provided to older workers as well, although not as much as to younger workers.

Contact your local Job Service Office for information on eligibility requirements or write to the Employment and Training Administration, Office of Special Targeted Programs.

3. OLDER WORKER PROGRAMS: For information on what's available in your community, contact Willis Martin, Chief, Division of Older Worker Programs at this address: Patrick Henry Building, 601 D Street, NW, Washington, D.C. 20213.

4. VETERAN'S EMPLOYMENT AND TRAINING SERVICE: Assists state Job Service offices and private contractors to provide counseling, job training and placement services.

5. WOMEN'S BUREAU: Its main function is to promote equality of employment opportunity, welfare in the workplace, and advancement opportunities for women workers. Also issues publications

which are free or of low cost. Among these are "Job Opportunities for Women in the 80's," "Women Are Under-represented as Managers and Skilled Crafts Workers," and "Handbook on Women Workers." Also send for a list of women's networks in your area.

PRESIDENT'S COMMITTEE ON EMPLOYMENT OF THE HANDICAPPED, Vanguard Building, 1111 20th Street, NW, Washington, DC, 20036. Issues a "Directory of Organizations Interested In The Handicapped" which lists voluntary and public agencies involved in the rehabilitation and employment of the handicapped.

STATE COMMISSIONS AND OFFICES ON AGING help persons 50 years of age and older. Contact your state's office for information on where to find career counseling, job training, and job placement services at little or no cost. Look in your phone book for the address of the nearest office.

WIDER OPPORTUNITIES FOR WOMEN, Inc. (W.O.W.) provides training for jobs traditionally held by men, career counseling for women in management and the professions, and job placement. Some centers charge a fee. It also publishes a "National Directory of Employment Programs for Women." Headquarters are at 1511 K Street, NW, Suite 700, Washington, DC 20006.

WOMEN IN MANAGEMENT (525 North Grant, Westmont, IL 60559) is a support network for women in professional and management jobs.

OTHER SOURCES OF HELP IN FINDING A JOB

RECRUITING AND EMPLOYMENT SERVICES: Recruiting firms differ from employment services in that they are paid by employers to find someone with special qualifications. They often raid rival companies for their most talented employees. As a rule, they seek you out; you don't go to them. However, some are known to keep a file of resumes sent to them by promising job seekers. Send in your resume and follow it up with a phone call to ask for a meeting. Better yet, ask someone you know who is in management to make the initial contact for you.

You can get a list of recruiting firms from the Association of Executive Search Consultants, Inc., 151 Railroad Avenue, Greenwich, CT. (phone 203-661-6606). (Don't let on that you are looking for a job.) Many firms place ads in the business

211

section of large city newspapers. Another source is Gale's "Directory of Associations." A copy of the "Executive Employment Guide" can be obtained by sending $3.25 to The American Management Association, 135 West 50th Street, New York, NY 10020.

COUNCIL FOR CAREER PLANNING (310 Madison Avenue, New York, NY 10017) issues booklets with samples of resumes and application letters. Send for a free brochure and price list.

U.S. OFFICE OF PERSONNEL MANAGEMENT deals with full and part-time Federal civil service jobs. Many of the jobs require passing a civil service examination. You can get information and application forms at your local Job Service office and at the local post office. Or, you may write to the U.S. Office of Personnel Management, P.O. Box 52, Washington, D.C. 20044 for information.

SUGGESTED READINGS

CAREER GUIDE TO PROFESSIONAL ORGANIZATIONS (Carroll Press, 1980) classifies thousands of organizations by occupational field.

DIRECTORY OF SPECIAL OPPORTUNITIES FOR WOMEN edited by Marth M. Doss (Garrett Park Press, 1981).

FINDING A JOB IN YOUR FIELD: A HANDBOOK FOR PH.D.'s AND M.A.'s by Rebecca Anthony and Gerald Roe (Peterson's Guides, 1985).

IS NETWORKING FOR YOU? A WORKING WOMAN'S ALTERNATIVE TO THE OLD BOY SYSTEM, by Barbara Stern (Prentice Hall, 1980).

LIBERAL ARTS POWER, by Burton J. Nadler (Peterson's Guides, 1985). A resume book for liberal arts graduates and others who have not trained for a specific job or profession.

NATIONAL DIRECTORY OF WOMEN'S EMPLOYMENT PROGRAMS published by Wider Opportunities for Women (W.O.W.), 1649 K Street, NW, Washington, DC 20006.

NETWORKING, by Mary Scott Welch (Warner Books, 1981).

The question, "Who ought to be boss?" is like asking, "Who ought to be tenor in the quartet?" Obviously, the man who can sing tenor.
— Henry Ford

THE PROFESSIONAL AND TRADE ASSOCIATION JOB FINDER: A DIRECTORY OF EMPLOYMENT RESOURCES OFFERED BY ASSOCIATIONS AND OTHER ORGANIZATIONS by Norman S. Feingold and Avis Nicholson (Garrett Park Press, 1983).

PROFESSIONAL RESUME/JOB SEARCH GUIDE, by Harold Dickhut (Prentice-Hall, 1981) contains resume samples for persons in specific business specialties (e.g., accounting, law, sales).

RESUME PREPARATION MANUAL: A STEP-BY-STEP GUIDE FOR WOMEN (Catalyst)

YOU CAN SELL ANYTHING BY TELEPHONE by Dr. Gary S. Goodman (Prentice-Hall)

WHAT TO DO WHEN YOU LOSE YOUR JOB is a 24-page booklet which offers advice on such topics as keeping your home, working out a survival budget, borrowing against insurance policies and applying for financial benefits. Send $1.00 and a stamped, self-addressed envelope to the Public Affairs Committee, 381 Park Avenue South, New York, NY 10016.

WORKING WOMAN is a monthly magazine with topics on a wide range of interest to women on their way up. There are no frills and fluff to this magazine; it's serious, well informed and a heavyweight in the world of business magazines. Single issues cost $2.50; a year's subscription can be had for $18. Write to WORKING WOMAN, P.O. Box 10132, Des Moines, IA 50340.

YES, YOU CAN! THE WORKING WOMAN'S GUIDE TO HER LEGAL RIGHTS, FAIR EMPLOYMENT AND EQUAL PAY by Emily B. Kirby (Prentice-Hall)

CAREER COUNSELING

Free or low cost career testing and counseling can be found in some public libraries, community agencies, adult education divisions of high schools, colleges, universities and state agencies. Look in the Yellow Pages of your phone book or ask the local librarian for help in locating a reputable counseling service.

Also look at the public library's collection of self-help books on choosing an appropriate career. After doing the exercises in chapter five of this book, or others you'll find in the library, you may not need professional help. However, some people prefer individual guidance from a career counseling professional. Furthermore, there are some psychological tests which can only be administered by a professional.

For-profit, private services generally ask you to sign a contract before any counseling begins. Take a copy home to study before you sign anything and make sure anything that is vaguely worded is clearly explained, in writing! Only after you have complete information on all the promised services and the length of time involved should you sign a contract.

Get a detailed list of all costs involved, too, or you may discover, too late, that several hundred dollars have been added to your bill simply for asking the counselor's opinion of your resume.

Ask about the counselor's training and experience and whether he/she belongs to a professional association. A counselor who is a member is more likely to be up-to-date in the profession. Furthermore, certain psychological tests can only be administered and interpreted by professional counselors.

It is unprofessional to give career counseling advice solely on the basis of written tests. Your work and educational background and your personal history should also be explored.

A reputable service should not promise, or even imply, to find you a good job.

Before enrolling in a career workshop, find out the size of the group beforehand. If it's too big, you won't get the personalized attention you may need.

Don't be put off by a high fee. It will be worth it if the expert counseling leads to a good career decision. Some of these services follow up on the progress of clients during the early stages of a new job to make sure they adjust well.

Some states require private counseling services to uphold the same regulations as employment agencies. This deters the unscrupulous operators. Consumer complaints were filed in 1983 against several New York agencies which charged as high as $8,000 for services which also guaranteed a good job. One of these simply helped clients prepare a resume and cover letter and gave them a list of employers to contact which the clients could have gotten themselves from sources listed here.

Check to see if any consumer complaints have been filed. Contact the Better Business Bureau or the Consumer Affairs Department of your city or county.

"The Directory of Approved Counseling Services" is an annual publication which lists accredited members of the International Association of Counseling Services (an affiliate of the American Personnel and Guidance Service). Be sure to get the current edition. If you can't find it in the local library, write to the Association at Two Skyline Plaza, 5203 Leesburg Pike, Falls Church, VA 22041.

BEHAVIORDYNE (994 San Antonio Road, Palo Alto, CA 94303) has a do-it-yourself kit of vocational tests which include the California Psychological Inventory and the Strong-Campbell Interest Inventory. Also included is information to help you decide which of 83 occupational areas you are most compatible with. After you mail back the results of your self-analysis and testing, the company sends you a report, a profile of your interests, and a workbook to help you decide on your career options.

CATALYST (250 Park Avenue South, New York, NY 10003) will send you a free brochure which lists accredited career counseling and placement centers in your state. It also issues a series of pamphlets and books on do-it-yourself career counseling, life planning and job search skills for women. Write for a free list.

COUNCIL FOR CAREER PLANNING (310 Madison Avenue, New York, NY 10017) is an affiliate of colleges and universities which provides career counseling, placement and various job opportunity resources. Projects include aid to disadvantaged women, minorities, older women and youth.

DISPLACED HOMEMAKER NETWORK also gives information on free or low-cost counseling and placement in or near your community. It serves older women who are re-entering the job market. Write to their headquarters at 1325 G Street, NW, Washington, DC 20005.

JOB SERVICE OFFICES in or near your community may still be offering career testing and counseling free of charge.

THE JOHNSON O'CONNOR RESEARCH FOUNDATION is a non-profit organization with centers in 16 major cities across the nation. The fee of $350 includes three sessions totalling 11 1/2 hours of individual testing of aptitudes, vocabulary and interests, followed by consultation on how to make an appropriate educational and career choice. There is a free session within a year of completing the program to ensure the choice was a happy one. For information write to the Foundation's headquarters at 11 East 62nd Street, New York, NY 10021 or phone 212-838-0550.

STATE VOCATIONAL REHABILITATION AGENCIES offer career counseling and placement services to people with handicaps. Some offer free literature on the job market and job-hunting tips for the handicapped. Look also in the public library and the local bookstore for job hunting books written especially for the handicapped.

WOMEN'S CENTERS AND ORGANIZATIONS: Many offer career counseling for little or no charge. See the network sources listed above.

SUGGESTED READINGS

CAREER APTITUDE TESTS (Arco Publishing, Inc.)

A COUNSELOR'S GUIDE TO OCCUPATIONAL INFORMATION (U.S. Department of Labor) lists a variety of career guidance publications issued by Federal agencies. You can order a copy from the Superintendent of Documents, U.S. Government Printing Office, Washington, DC 20402. Your library probably has a copy.

THE HIDDEN JOB MARKET FOR THE 80's, by Tom Jackson and Davidyne Mayleas (Times Books, 1981), includes about 50 quizzes to help you match your strengths to job families.

IT'S YOUR FUTURE! CATALYST'S CAREER GUIDE FOR HIGH SCHOOL GIRLS (Peterson's Guides, 1985).

MATCHING PERSONAL AND JOB CHARACTERISTICS (U.S. Department of Labor) includes an easy-to-use chart for comparing your background and personality with the characteristics of over 280 occupations. Write to Consumer Information Center, Dept. H., Pueblo, CO 81009.

WHAT COLOR IS YOUR PARACHUTE?, by Richard N. Bolles (Ten Speed Press, 1985) is a best seller. It includes the "Quick Job Hunting Map" and discusses how to deal with rejection, where to get help, who has the power to hire you, and more.

WHAT TO DO WITH THE REST OF YOUR LIFE: THE CATALYST CAREER GUIDE FOR WOMEN IN THE '80s (Simon & Schuster, 1981).

WHERE DO I GO FROM HERE WITH MY LIFE?, by John C. Crystal and Richard N. Bolles (Ten Speed Press, 1981), is a workbook for job hunters and career changers written by two of the leaders in this field.

UPGRADE YOUR SKILLS ❖ LEARN NEW SKILLS

Contact THE ADULT EDUCATION DIVISION of your local school board or the school superintendent's office for information about courses and services in your community for adults.

EMPLOYMENT AND TRAINING ADMINISTRATION, U.S. Department of Labor. Contact the regional office nearest you or write to the headquarters for the address--601 D Street, NW, Washington, DC 20530.

NATIONAL ASSOCIATION OF TRADE AND TECHNICAL SCHOOLS, Office of Public Information, 2021 K Street, NW, Washington, DC 20006. Send for the "Directory of Accredited Private Trade and Technical Schools."

NATIONAL EDUCATION ASSOCIATION OF THE UNITED STATES, 1201 16th Street, NW, Washington, DC 20036 (for general inquiries).

NATIONAL HOME STUDY COUNCIL, 1601 18th Street, NW, Washington, DC 20009. Send for the "Directory of Home Study Schools." It also lists the courses offered by each school.

POST-SECONDARY EDUCATION PROGRAMS FOR DEAF AND OTHER HANDI-CAPPED, U.S. Department of Education, Room 3121, Donohoe Building, 400 Maryland Avenue, SW, Washington, DC 20201.

Look in the phone book for your STATE'S EDUCATION SERVICES (such as the following New York State services). They may be listed under the same or similar titles:

    Department of Labor
    Cultural Education Center
    Office of Apprenticeship Training
    Office of Vocational Rehabilitation
    Higher Education Services Corporation

Office of Independent Study (home study)
Higher Education Opportunities Program
Office of Non-Collegiate Sponsored Education
University Without Walls (home study college courses)

Your LOCAL LIBRARY has a wealth of information on adult education. It may also have college catalogues which contain a complete description of course offerings, tuition and other costs, extra-curricular activities in your field, and more.

Ask for information on independent or home study if you want to study for credit at home or in a nearby locale.

Also ask for information on education sponsored and paid for by private companies. Believe it or not, more money is spent on job-related education and training by private industry than by the entire educational establishment in the U.S.

SUGGESTED READINGS

GUIDE TO INDEPENDENT STUDY THROUGH CORRESPONDENCE INSTRUCTION, by the National University Extension Association. Order from Peterson's Guides, Book Order Department, Box 978, Edison, NJ 08817.

GUIDE TO TWO-YEAR COLLEGES by Kim R. Kaye (Peterson's Guides).

GUIDE TO FOUR-YEAR COLLEGES BY Kim R. Kaye (Petersons's Guides). Contains complete college profiles.

HOW TO GET CREDIT FOR WHAT YOU KNOW: ALTERNATIVE ROUTES TO EDUCATIONAL CREDIT is a free brochure issued by the Women's Bureau, U.S. Department of Labor, Washington, DC 20210.

ON-CAMPUS, OFF-CAMPUS DEGREE PROGRAMS FOR PART-TIME STUDENTS, by the National University Extension Service (Peterson's Guides).

TIPS ON HOME STUDY SCHOOLS, by the Council of Better Business Bureaus. Call your local BBB or write to the Council at 1150 17th Street, NW, Washington, DC 20036. A must for anyone who is considering taking home study or correspondence courses.

WHO OFFERS PART-TIME DEGREE PROGRAMS? by Kim R. Kaye (Peterson's Guides).

HOW TO PASS EXAMS

HOW TO BEAT TEST ANXIETY AND SCORE HIGHER ON YOUR EXAMS, by James Divine and David Kylen (Barron).

HOW TO MASTER TEST TAKING by Fred A. Anderson (Skills Improvement).

HOW TO PASS EMPLOYMENT TESTS by Arthur Liebers (Arco).

HOW TO TAKE AND PASS SIMPLE TESTS FOR CIVIL SERVICE JOBS by Solomon Wiener (Monarch Press).

TEST PREPARATION FOR PROFESSIONAL AND ADMINISTRATIVE POSITIONS IN THE FEDERAL SERVICE (Arco Publishing, Inc.)
   Also look into Arco's many guides for passing examinations for various occupations (e.g., "Allied Health Professions Admissions Test").

HOW TO ACHIEVE THE LOOK OF SUCCESS

CLOTHES AND GROOMING

DIRECTORY OF PERSONAL IMAGE CONSULTANTS (Editorial Services, Brooklyn Heights, NY 11201, 1985 edition).

THE EXECUTIVE LOOK: HOW TO GET IT, HOW TO KEEP IT BY Mortimer Levitt (Atheneum)

THE WOMAN'S DRESS FOR SUCCESS BOOK by John T. Molloy (Warner Books) is a best seller

COMMUNICATE WITH IMPACT

Write to CATALYST for the following publications for women (also helpful to men): "Attitudes: Male/Female" and "Assertiveness Training".

CHANGE YOUR VOICE/CHANGE YOUR LIFE: A QUICK, SIMPLE PLAN FOR FINDING YOUR NATURAL, DYNAMIC VOICE by Dr. Morton Cooper (MacMillan, 1984).

HOW TO TALK WELL by James F. Bender (McGraw Hill)

MAKE THE MOST OF YOUR BEST: A COMPLETE PROGRAM FOR PRESENTING YOURSELF & YOUR IDEAS WITH CONFIDENCE AND AUTHORITY by Dorothy Sarnoff (Doubleday, 1981).

THE PROFESSIONAL IMAGE by Susan Bixler, a corporate consultant, offers advice to men and women on how to look and carry themselves (Putnam)

REDUCE STRESS AND INCREASE SELF-CONFIDENCE

THE CONFIDENCE QUOTIENT: 10 STEPS TO CONQUER SELF-DOUBT by Meryle Gellman and Diane Gage (World Almanac Publications, 1984).

THE GREAT AMERICAN SUCCESS STORY: FACTORS THAT AFFECT ACHIEVEMENT by George Gallup, Jr. and Alec M. Gallup (Dow Jones-Irwin, 1985)--includes profiles of successful people from all walks of life.

HOW TO SURVIVE GETTING FIRED AND WIN by Jerry Cowle (Warner Books, 1980).

A NEW BEGINNING: HOW YOU CAN CHANGE YOUR LIFE THROUGH COGNITIVE THERAPY by Dr. Gary Emery (Simon & Schuster)

SHYNESS by Philip G. Zimbardo and Shirley L. Radl (Jove Publications, 1984).

STRESS AND THE ART OF BIOFEEDBACK by Barbara B. Brown (Harper-Row, 1977).

THE VISCOTT METHOD: A REVOLUTIONARY PROGRAM FOR SELF ANALYSIS AND SELF-UNDERSTANDING by David Viscott, M.D. (Houghton Mifflin, 1985). A method based on confiding into a tape recorder and analyzing the results to identify strengths and weaknesses, define goals, and perform exercises to enhance self-esteem. Dr. Viscott is a psychiatrist.

JOB INTERVIEW: The excruciating process during which personnel officers separate the wheat from the chaff -- then hire the chaff.
—Jim Fisk & Robert Barron
(Buzzwords: The Official MBA Dictionary,
1983, Wallaby/Simon & Shuster)

INDEX

221